Learning the Business of Life

Gramey Browne

Xtreme Business Concepts, Inc.
P.O Box 971
Oakland, Florida 34760
www.myxbc.com

Learning the Business of Life

Publisher:
Xtreme Business Concepts, Inc.
P.O Box 971
Oakland, Florida 34760
Email: info@grameybrowne.com
Website: www.grameybrowne.com

ISBN: 978-1-963177-67-1
Gramey Browne© 2024

All rights reserved. No part of this book may be reproduced by artificial intelligence or transmitted in any form or by any means, electronic or mechanical, including photocopying, recording, or by any information storage and retrieval system, without permission in writing from the publisher. Brief quotations embodied in critical articles and reviews may be used without prior written consent of the author or publisher.

CONTENTS

Introduction i
Starting the Entrepreneurial Journey iii
Discovery viii
About Me xii
The Contractor 1
Cleaning the Yard 5
The Altar Boy 9
The Transition 12
The Mentor 21
The Time 30
The Five-Year Plan 35
Bullying 39
Cost of Living 57
Goodbye and Hello 65
Pursuing the Business of Life 77
Browne's Wisdom 80
Reflective Insights 82
Thank You Notes 85

Introduction

Overview of Memoir Goals and Themes

This memoir traces my entrepreneurial journey from childhood origins to adulthood success. The tales aim to transport readers through pivotal moments that molded my work ethic and lit an inner fire that's still burning brightly today.

By sharing stories from my formative years, my goal is to pass along hard-won lessons that will inspire you—and through you, many others—to take the practical steps contained in these pages to get you where you want to go in life.

You'll meet colorful island mentors who nurtured my talents amidst tropical backdrops. Follow along through stories of happiness and heartaches across the waves to distant shores. Witness my evolution from a wide-eyed boy selling prints door-to-door into a determined man forging my own path.

While a modest beginning selling wares to friends might seem small, the same passion and enthusiasm empowered my business ventures. By sharing these memories, I hope to spark fellow dreamers worldwide.

The memoir shares universal themes we all face of persevering through hardship, learning from mistakes, and recognizing the power of community.

If my unlikely journey can open doors for even one person, inspire a fellow striver, or build common ground, then it will serve its core purpose.

The world needs more diverse voices from all walks of life to light the entrepreneurial spark within us.

I welcome you to share in these lessons learned along the sea about an island boy's pursuit of success during his early years that molded him into the man he is today.

Starting the Entrepreneurial Journey

Learning Life Lessons along the Way

I believe the only real limitations in business and in life can be overcome by your imagination and determination to succeed. If you're willing to work harder and smarter than those around you on a consistent basis, your possibilities in life are truly limitless.

My sole purpose in writing this book is to share my early life experiences that will inspire you to tap into your own entrepreneurial spirit. The stories contained within these pages take you through some of my earliest childhood business ventures. Even though I was young, there were several jobs I took starting around age 12 that shaped who I was as I began to chart my financial course.

By sharing my entrepreneurial journey, I hope to encourage you to set financial mileposts for yourself and embark on a rewarding journey of your own.

You'll also learn about a wise mentor who saw potential in me that I had not yet recognized in myself and guided me in what he called *"the business of life."* Now I aim to pay that guidance forward by empowering the next generation.

With age comes nuanced perspectives I lacked in my bold youth. I hope my stories will spark new ideas, provide wisdom, and bring more balance, fullness, and meaning to your life.

Through the ups and downs of my early business pursuits and life lessons, one constant theme was reinforced that steadied me through life: the enduring power of perseverance. Good things rarely come easily—or quickly.

The path was not always smooth, yet adversity built grit to overcome obstacles. My sincere wish is that my stories will motivate you to unlock your own potential and awaken your inner sleeping giants of relentless determination and resourcefulness.

By bravely taking first one step and then another, embracing uncertainties, and learning from your past mistakes, you can chart your own fulfilling path for your future. The first step is often both the easiest and the hardest—simply making the decision to begin. Once you take that all-important first step, you're on a path to financial freedom and security that will pay dividends for the rest of your life.

Now in my fifties and reflecting back on my youth, the life lessons learned, and entrepreneurial career decisions I made along the way, I've come to some conclusions. Here are two key sets of takeaways.

Lessons I learned in life:

1. Comparing yourself to others leads to jealousy and a lack of self-love and empathy. Instead, reflect on how far you've come.

2. The grass often appears greener on the other side, and sometimes that's true—it is. However, at other times it's just an illusion. The "grass" is artificial or a weed-filled mirage. What looks appealing from afar can easily be disappointing up close.

3. Fortunately, unlike in sports, there are very few times in life with clear-cut winners and losers. Someone else's success doesn't equal your failure. We must each be free to follow our own path with its unique ups and downs. Don't view life as a competition to be won, especially at the expense of someone else losing. We can all achieve our goals and find fulfillment in different ways and on different timelines. Encourage the progress of others and celebrate their success.

4. Even though life is a gift to be cherished, we earn success through hard work. Free handouts may come with unspoken debts, unmet expectations, and other unforeseen consequences. Harboring secret fantasies of marrying royalty, winning the lottery, or inheriting a fortune from a distant relative are just dreams for most people. Focus on achievable goals, and then take concrete steps that will help you get there.

5. The only yardstick that matters is your own. Life isn't about keeping up with the Joneses. The most important person you must measure up to is yourself. Avoid wasting time dwelling on thoughts of envy

and entitlement. Instead, by having realistic expectations, humility, and perseverance, you can find true meaning and contentment in your work and in your personal life.

This outlook on life helped me succeed in my early years, and I know it will be effective for you too.

Lessons I learned in business:

1. If you're not committed to a project for the long term, carefully evaluate any risks you're taking in the short term. Statistically, 80% of new businesses fail within the first five years.

2. Every investment carries some degree of risk. Never invest money you cannot afford to lose.

3. Savings accounts and CDs are essentially risk-free 99.98% of the time, offering guaranteed returns.

4. Your physical and mental health are your greatest assets. Without your health, you won't be able to fully enjoy your wealth. Prioritize investing in your overall wellness each and every day.

5. When considering starting a business, begin by testing your product or service on your friends, family, and neighbors. Use their honest feedback to refine your offering and iron out mistakes before a broader launch.

The road to success in business is filled with many twists and turns. However, by carefully managing risk, avoiding common pitfalls, and staying nimble, you can dramatically increase your chances of joining the winning 20% of businesses that thrive past the five-year mark.

Now let's get into the specifics of how I learned these key lessons firsthand.

Discovery

Learning Business Concepts Young

When I had my first taste of the world of entrepreneurship, I was only in fifth grade, and what it taught me was that doing business does not have to be complicated. With dedication and some basic yet clever ideas, anyone can get started.

I was only 12 years old at the time in a fifth-grade class called "Principles of Business." I still remember the lesson: John bought an apple for one guilder and proceeded to sell it for 1.10 guilders. John had made a 0.10-guilder profit, which illustrated the fundamental principle of business.

The goal of any replicable business process is to complete the same or a similar rewarding transaction over and over again. If you can repeat profitable transactions every second of every minute of every day, week after week, month after month, year after year, you exponentially increase your chances of earning a substantial return on the money you invested in operating a thriving business.

While the concept might seem oversimplified, the class taught me the essence of a business deal: find a product people will want to buy, locate a paying customer, and sell the item at a profit. That's it!

Despite what most people think, a business does not require a fancy storefront, rich investors, or employees to get it off the ground. In fact, all it really takes is a good idea, a product that's in demand, a willing customer, and the ability to close that crucial first transaction.

At the end of the course, I walked away feeling empowered, filled with confidence that I could one day run a successful business of my own. Armed with new enthusiasm, motivation, and entrepreneurial drive, I could not wait for an opportunity to give it a try myself.

It was that very weekend, when I was visiting a friend's house, that I noticed an eye-catching plaque on the wall of their living room. It read:

> **When you come here,**
> **What you see here,**
> **What you hear here,**
> **What you think about here,**
> **Leave it here;**
> **otherwise, don't come back here.**

I thought this was an item that would appeal to lots of people—in short, a great place to start. I asked my friend if I could borrow the plaque, explaining that I wanted to make photocopies of it at the library. He agreed to let me take it down.

I had 5 guilders in my pocket, enough to make 20 copies at 25 cents each. I could barely contain my excitement and hurried the entire walk to the library and the whole way home with a silly grin plastered across my face.

After returning the plaque to the wall so his mom wouldn't notice it was borrowed, I wasted no time and made a small profit going door to door selling the copies for 1 guilder each.

After selling the first 19 copies, I used the last copy and the money I had earned to make over 100 additional copies—and sold every last one. I could not stop smiling with the cash filling my pockets!

But more meaningful than that, I had proven to my 12-year-old self that I could conduct real business transactions.

While this was only a simple fifth-grade business class, it planted an important seed, showing me that business need not be complicated. This firsthand experience taught me that with dedication and creative thinking, anyone can get a business off the ground.

The empowerment and entrepreneurial spark I gained from those formative lessons stuck with me over the years. Though I lacked money and resources back then, I realized that business barriers often exist mainly in our minds. When we get creative and take action, possibilities open up.

The class built my confidence to give business a try myself, setting me on my path to pursue my passions and become an entrepreneur. No matter how high I climbed over the years, I never forgot the excitement of those simple beginnings and the foundational business concepts mastered in the fifth grade.

Consider starting a business as a teenager; living with your parents can be very advantageous. They may even be willing to pitch in and cover some or all of your startup costs if you pitch it properly.

Here are some questions:

1. Did you ever have any business ideas or try starting small ventures as a kid? What did you do?
2. Were there moments in childhood when you realized you had an entrepreneurial drive or spirit? What sparked it?
3. Did your parents or other adults nurture and encourage your early business ideas? If so, how?
4. What core concepts around buying, selling, and profiting did you grasp at a young age from life experiences?
5. If you have a child who shows entrepreneurial interests, how would you foster their development in those areas?

About Me

Growing Up in St. Eustatius

I was born in Saint Kitts and Nevis in the late 1960s. I am the youngest of three boys my mother had from previous relationships. I was the baby of our family until my sister came along much later when I was already 11 years old.

In the 1970s, my mother Emelyne married a gentleman 16 years her senior named Monty Courtar from the small Caribbean Island of St. Eustatius.

I was six years old when we migrated there as a family, and I lived on St. Eustatius until the mid-1980s. My two older brothers lived with their father on the island of St. Lucia, so I was raised like an only child by my mother and stepfather.

Our home was a humble yet bustling one with a backyard full of animals cared for by my stepdad. He had a true talent for husbandry and livestock. We raised goats, sheep, chickens, a cow, calves, and even a stubborn donkey.

Among my daily chores was herding these animals. Each morning before school, I'd round up our motley crew and usher them out to pasture. Then in the afternoons, I was tasked with bringing them back in again before sundown.

Some of the young goats and lambs had to be bottle-fed when they were still small and weak. Not surprisingly, I grew attached to the animals, considering them part of our family until the inevitable day they were sent to slaughter.

Caring for this menagerie taught me responsibility from a young age, along with the virtues of patience and perseverance. I learned that progress and growth happen gradually, one step at a time. But with consistency and commitment, you'll reach your goals in due course.

These insights would serve me well in later entrepreneurial pursuits, where grit and tenacity are key.

I was generally a well-behaved little boy, or so I'd like to believe! As a child, I loved going to concerts, sporting events, and the movie theater. I spent relatively carefree days glued to the television at times, watching professional wrestling and shows like *Starsky and Hutch, The A-Team, The Six Million Dollar Man, MacGyver, Man from Atlantis, Hawaii Five-O,* and *The Incredible Hulk.*

Measuring only 11.8 square miles (approximately 21 square kilometers) in area, the island of St. Eustatius, nicknamed "Statia," also called the "Golden Rock" and "Historic Gem," is part of the breathtakingly beautiful Dutch Caribbean, which includes Aruba, Bonaire, Curaçao, Saba, and Saint Maarten.

Located in the northern leeward islands southeast of the U.S. Virgin Islands and northwest of St. Kitts, St. Eustatius is known for its hiking, fishing, diving, natural beauty, and historic landmarks. Like any tropical destination, of course, you can also come to relax and do nothing.

Statia is famous for its "First Salute" to an American vessel, a historic event signifying early recognition of U.S. independence. On November 16, 1776, the *Andrew Doria*, an American merchant ship upgraded to a warship by the Continental Navy (later to become the U.S. Navy), received a cannon salute from Fort Oranje on Statia. Islanders remember this occasion with great pride. The "First Salute," commemorated annually on November 16th, is "National Statia Day," also known as "Statia America Day."

During my childhood in the 1970s, the population of Statia was only about 2,400 people—small enough that everyone knew each other. Even though the population has grown over the years, I believe that a tight-knit sense of community remains.

Growing up on Statia, when someone needed help, islanders were always willing to lend a hand. However, any misbehavior quickly got back to my mother, which often resulted in my punishment. The phrase "it takes a village to raise a child" certainly rang true in this instance.

My stepfather was a kind, good-looking gentleman and a man of few words. When he heard a good joke, he would belt out a hearty laugh until the tears were rolling down his face. His laughter was infectious; others would start laughing just watching and hearing him.

Learning the Business of Life

Monty was a skilled workman with his hands and a jack-of-all-trades when it came to projects involving carpentry, masonry, and plumbing; he was even proficient in electrical wiring. He was one of the go-to men on the island. I remember him building barstools and tables for two of the popular local bars.

For himself, he built a fishing boat, fish traps, and even a stone oven in our yard to bake fresh bread. If Monty didn't know how to do something himself, he always knew someone who did or who could point him in the right direction. One way or another, he would get the job done.

I loved playing checkers and dominoes with my stepdad growing up. He was a capable opponent—competitive and not one to let me win easily. If I wanted to win, I had to beat him fair and square, which did happen occasionally, and it felt so satisfying!

Monty had six children from a previous marriage before he met and married my mother, who already had three kids of her own. Monty and my mom were married for more than 35 years. He was truly a man of commitment and family. He embraced the role of husband, provider, and protector of his family.

My mom was a tall, formidable woman at 6 feet and weighing 200 pounds, while Monty was just 5'6" and 150 pounds. When they stood together, she towered over him!

Remarkably, as I write this in November 2023, my 94-year-old stepfather holds the title of the oldest man on Statia. He will turn 95 this December. To describe this incredible man in one sentence: George Monty Courtar is a man of great character and a giant among men.

My mother Emelyne was a stay-at-home mom and the disciplinarian of our family. She did not spare the rod and spoil this child. When sending me to the supermarket, she would spit on the ground and declare, "You better be back before this dry!"

She also walked me to school at the beginning of the school year in third and fourth grade—just to remind me that she knew precisely how long it took to get there and back. This was one of her ways of keeping me in line.

My mom had two stern rules:

1. Don't let anyone come to the house complaining about you.

2. Never bring a note home from the teacher asking her to come to school, or else she'll show up with a belt.

I learned this lesson the hard way. Once in third grade, my teacher explained to my mom that I was a good student, but I talked a lot in class and was at times disruptive. That was the reason for the remark in the behavior box on my report card: "Talks too much."

Right there on the spot, my mom took off a slipper and gave me four hard smacks on the backside, warning me that I would get the rest when we got home. I dreaded every minute of that 15-minute walk home.

After that day, I made sure to be on my best behavior and keep my mouth shut in class! The threat of incurring my mother's wrath was enough to keep me in line.

To describe her in one line: Emelyne Courtar Brown commands respect and is still a force to be reckoned with, no matter the situation, place, or person.

I did not know my biological father at all growing up. My mother spoke about him in unfavorable terms, yet I still had an interest in meeting him as a child. It wasn't until I was 27 years old that I flew to St. Kitts and met the man in person for the first time. We had a conversation lasting around 20 minutes.

Afterward, I walked away, thinking to myself, "This is a man I never need to speak to again." Our brief encounter told me everything I needed to know. I had been raised just fine without him in my life.

Here are some questions:

1. What memories do you have of older role models and mentors from your childhood who had an impact on you?

2. Did you grow up in a tight-knit community? What was memorable about it?

3. What influence did your parents or caregivers have in shaping your values and approach to life?

4. Were there any tales or legendary figures from your hometown who captured your imagination as a child?

5. If you have kids, what important life lessons and values do you hope to pass on to them?

The Contractor

Working Construction After School

After selling copies of the plaque and getting a taste of independence, I wanted to start earning my own money. At home, there was no such thing as a weekly or monthly allowance. The sum total of my compensation included room and board and use of the appliances.

There was a contractor who had a woodshop across from my family's house. I asked him if I could have a job cleaning up his construction sites to earn some pocket money. He said he couldn't hire me, but he could give me a subcontractor job. I didn't know what that word meant, but it sounded like an exciting role!

It would be my job to remove all the nails from plywood and 2x4 planks of lumber and then separate them into piles—short and long 2x4s in one pile, small and large plywood in another.

He offered to pay me 60 guilders per home site. I agreed, and we shook hands to seal the deal. I would work after school when the other workers went home.

I was excited to start, but I needed tools—at the very least, a hammer and a crowbar. For the first week, I borrowed the tools I needed from my stepdad. As soon as I earned my first pay, I purchased tools of my very own.

Although I had money saved, I would never have used it for that purpose—money already saved was only to be used as a last resort. With income on the way, I used the new money I was earning to meet the new job requirements.

The contractor was building 25 government-funded, low-income houses. He was about four house sites in when I started. For cleaning each home site, I received 60 guilders—about 33 U.S. dollars.

At first glance, it seemed like a lot of work, but I went every day after school and finished all four sites inside of one week. The contractor loved my work and said he could give me more assignments if I was up for it.

My next job consisted of cleaning and removing formwork from water cisterns after they were poured. I had to wait about two weeks for the poured concrete to set, then climb through an opening about 30 inches square and go down 5–6 feet deep.

I would knock out the forms, beams, and plywood, then toss them out of the cistern. Next, I would clean out any leftover debris and dirt, remove all the nails from the wood, and organize it alongside each house. I poured water on the cistern floor before sweeping to keep dust down. Then down in that semi-dark concrete box I went, with a wet cloth tied around my nose and mouth to filter out dust.

This was hard work, but I was still excited to be doing real construction jobs. I was paid 150 guilders per cistern and felt rich. Selling copies of the plaque earned me lots of coins, but this construction job paid real money—the folding kind!

As each new house was built, I removed nails from the wood and organized everything for reuse as well as cleaned the cisterns. I convinced a school friend to help me, and I paid him 50 guilders as an employee. It was very exciting; I felt like a real businessman and manager.

My contractor used to tell me, "Remember, son, a job is nothing but work. If you don't want to work, don't get a job." That saying stuck with me. I often repeat it when I hear people complain about working too hard.

Here are some jobs you can do in your neighborhood as a young teen after school to earn money:

- Pack bags at grocery stores
- Wash cars
- Clean up construction sites
- Walk dogs
- Babysit

Here are some questions:

1. Did you ever take on jobs or side work as a kid or teen to earn your own money? What motivated you?

2. When did you get your first "real" job with a regular salary? How did it feel?

3. What early work experiences helped shape your perspectives on the value of hard work and earning money?

4. As a kid, did you get an allowance, or did you need to work for spending money? What impact did that have?

5. Looking back, what do you think gave you your strong work ethic? Or what experiences instilled that in you?

Cleaning the Yard

Neighborhood Landscaping Business

From the time I was as young as eight years old, I had a savings account and a piggy bank. My mom would take me to the bank to deposit 10 to 30 guilders regularly. I realized early on that money disappears when it's spent. You can't have the money and the things you buy at the same time, which would be like having your cake and eating it too. So, earning and saving became more important than spending.

My mom always advised me to save a little or a lot and at least half of what I earned from any job. Later in life, I learned that "cash creates opportunities." In business, you need a financial cushion for the times when things don't go as planned. There's an old saying about money: "It's always better to have and not need than to need and not have." This wisdom guided me from a young age.

My third business venture was yard cleaning, or basic landscaping as it's known these days. Our island scrubs were sandy and wild grass plots, not tidy lawns. Working at home, I had to hack away at bushes with a machete.

Passersby took notice and asked if I'd clear their yards too. Soon I had 10 or more neighborhood yards to maintain. I was especially popular among the seniors. I earned 60 guilders or more per project. My only investment was a machete costing less than 50 guilders.

Even though I hadn't planned to, I became a young handyman—washing patios, clearing storage areas, and cleaning yards. This taught me business skills beyond landscaping, things like customer service, scheduling, and negotiating prices.

After consistently working weekends doing yard jobs at age 13, I relished having my own money to go to the movies or buy treats like burgers, ice cream, and candy. On one of my shopping sprees, I purchased a pair of Bruce Lee shoes, Fila sneakers, a Polo shirt, and jeans. I felt so mature and independent.

The task of juggling different jobs excited me, although it left little time for sports. I often wished there were more hours in the day! But I was motivated to work hard for the taste of freedom and adulthood my earnings provided. My modest upbringing made earning my own money even more empowering.

Once, I was hired to clean the yard for a supermarket owner who had me working alongside his sons loading stock. One son asked if I was getting paid for the work and seemed surprised when I said yes. For them, these were unpaid "chores," while I saw a return value for my efforts. Like their parents, my parents didn't pay for household chores.

While it may seem like routine teenage work, my early job removing nails and cleaning construction sites taught me invaluable lessons. Most important, it showed me the direct relationship between hard work and earned rewards.

I quickly grasped that services or skills I could provide had tangible value others would pay for. This built an empowering sense of independence and pride at a young age.

Beyond the money earned, I gained hands-on skills assembling and repairing things around job sites. This experience paved the way to pursue construction as a career later on. Looking back, those formative years spent laboring after school played a major role in shaping my tenacious work ethic and business mindset.

My first boss drove home to me that work requires effort, but effort delivers returns. I carry this understanding today in my ventures and strive to pass on its wisdom. For any young person, recognizing that your time and talents have worth unlocks potential. With that key insight, you can begin building the foundation for your own enterprises and independence.

Here are some questions:

1. Did you have any childhood jobs or ways you made your own spending money? What motivated you to do them?

2. Were you required to save a portion of the money you earned or received as a kid? What money lessons stuck with you?

3. Did your parents pay you for doing chores around the house? Do you plan to do the same or something else with your own kids?

4. What was the first major purchase you saved up to make with your own money? How proud were you when you got it?

5. If you could start any small neighborhood business today, what would it be? What is it about the idea that gets you excited?

The Altar Boy

Role of Religion in Upbringing

I had an eclectic religious upbringing—attending a Catholic school while also attending various churches, including Seventh-Day Adventist, Methodist, Apostolic Faith, and later, the Baha'i faith. My christening and confirmation took place at the Anglican church, while my first holy communion was at the Catholic church. I served as an altar boy for both the Catholic and Anglican churches.

While church attendance was mandatory at home, I valued the enriching experience. I attended every church on our small island while growing up, even reading the Jehovah's Witness magazine at home.

One of my favorite biblical passages is John 3:16: "For God so loved the world...." To this day, I am a sincere believer in Jesus dying for my sins and the promise of Him going to prepare a place for me in heaven.

One of my brothers became a pastor and gospel recording artist with his wife. Though I never felt called to the ministry myself, I sought relationships with women of faith. My wife and I have passed these Christian beliefs on to our daughter through bedtime prayers and rituals rooted in family traditions.

From childhood, I learned the bedtime and mealtime prayers my mother taught us all.

- At bedtime: "In my little bed I lay, Heavenly Father, hear my cry. God protects us through the night. Keep us safe till morning light."
- And again in the morning: "Thank you, Lord, for sparing our lives to see another day."

  Before meals, we would pray, "Thank you, Lord, for this food we are about to eat. Please bless the hands that prepared it. May it nourish and strengthen our bodies and keep us healthy."

I've shared these cherished beliefs with my wife and daughter, who are also devout Christians. The simple act of praying together roots us in the Christian faith adopted by my ancestors generations ago. Traditions like these provide comfort and meaning that withstand the test of time.

Here are some questions:

1. What role did faith and religion play in your upbringing? Do you have any special memories associated with your childhood place of worship?

2. Were there any religious rituals, prayers, or practices that held special meaning in your family through the generations? What memories do they evoke?

3. How have your faith and spirituality evolved from childhood into adulthood?

4. Are there any passages from religious texts that have stuck with you since you were young? Why did they resonate?

5. Have your core values and worldview been shaped by early religious influences? In what ways?

The Transition

Moving Abroad and Adapting

Before the mid-1980s, students on Statia had to immigrate to another island for secondary school because there were no options locally. The government subsidized most costs for Dutch citizens attending school abroad. Many of my classmates went to St. Maarten, Curaçao, or Aruba. However, my lack of Dutch citizenship limited my opportunities, as my parents would have to pay full price.

Still, I was excited by the prospect of leaving Statia like my peers—going to a new island, making new friends, and being immersed in a different culture.

I was sent to St. Croix to live with my mom's close friend, Aunty Margaret, with the hope of attending school there. I spent the last two weeks of summer vacation getting acclimated, but as August came and went, I did not start school as planned. This great opportunity had fallen through.

Aunty Margaret's house sat on about two acres of lush land. It was a nice, cozy two-bedroom house of around 1,400 square feet. The house was situated toward the front of the property, while fruit trees flourished abundantly in the back.

Depending on the season, there were sugar apples, guineps (Spanish limes), papaya, mangoes, avocados, bananas, and more—all dropping fresh from the trees. There were so many, I couldn't possibly eat them all, though I tried my best!

Of course, that's when my entrepreneurial instincts kicked in. Guess what I did? Oh yes... I started selling!

I would harvest the ripe fruit, fill a soda crate, and sell it at the local ballpark. I just couldn't stand watching good fruit go to waste when I could earn money selling the leftover abundance. Plus, I simply could not resist the urge to put my business ideas into action.

My aunt was busy working two jobs, so on most days I was left home on my own, which was not an issue having grown up an only child. She phoned me every day to make sure I was okay.

There was a park and playground nearby where I played basketball, volleyball, checkers, and dominoes with other boys, both my age and older. The house had cable TV and a stereo system for entertainment.

I knew how to cook several of my favorite meals, including white or curry rice with chicken wings or stew beef and macaroni and cheese with hot dogs. I would go to the market to buy plantains to complement my meals, along with sweet potatoes, yams, carrots, and breadfruit for soup.

I was very self-sufficient as a young teenager. I could wash clothes, iron, clean the house, and cook. As a child, I helped my mom with chores like washing clothes by hand using a washboard then rinsing and hanging them on the clothesline to dry in the sun. I remember racing back to grab them when it rained, or going before sundown to collect them.

When ironing, my mom always warned, "Iron the clothing, not your fingers." I even had to help clean the house and dust, sweep, and mop every week.

Doing chores taught me responsibility and built my confidence in being able to care for myself—skills I was putting to use.

My mom had three rules about food and cooking:

1. Boys need to know how to cook so their future wives can't starve them.
2. My sister needed to learn to cook so she could feed and keep her future husband.
3. If you didn't like what she cooked, you were free to cook your own food.

One day, I was craving my mom's dumplings, so I decided to try making them myself for the first time. I prepared the flour and when the water started boiling, I dropped my hand-molded dough into the pot. My plan was to cook plenty of dumplings—some to fry the next day for breakfast with eggs and a hot dog and some to eat that same day with stew chicken.

Yet about five minutes after adding the dumplings, the pot started boiling over—the dumplings had expanded to the size of the entire pot! I panicked, having never seen that happen when my mom made them. So, I added more water because most of it had boiled over.

By then, the dumplings were the size of my face! I turned off the stove and called my mom to tell her what happened. She asked what ingredients I had put in it. I said, "Flour, salt, cornmeal, oil, and baking powder."

My mother laughed at my mistake for a few seconds, then said, "Boy, what's wrong with you? You don't put baking powder in dumplings!" I had confused part of the dumpling recipe with the johnnycake recipe.

That cooking mishap turned out to be a blessing in disguise. I fried the rest of the johnnycake dough and started a proper dumpling batch. I had plenty of food for lunch, dinner, and the next day's breakfast, lunch, and dinner. Trust me—they tasted so good!

Have you ever tried peanut butter and jelly on warm johnnycake? Or hot johnnycake with a hot dog and melted cheese? If not, add it to your bucket list. But brace yourself for the intense flavors and textures hitting your mouth all at once. Then hope your stomach understands the food coming down from your mouth!

Sometimes I spent long weekends at Aunty Lorene's home, which was about a 30-minute bus ride away. She had a much bigger house, along with two sons and two daughters.

Her eldest son was away serving in the U.S. Army. Though we never spoke or met, seeing photos of him in uniform inspired me to become a soldier myself one day. It would be another eight years before I joined the Dutch Marines and lived on the Marine base in Curaçao, but the seed was planted.

As a Marine, we were taught that there are constantly surprises requiring adaptation, and learned to always have backup plans ready, pivoting when conditions change. I carried this attitude into my career.

On my journey, failure was not an option. Being resilient and learning flexibility from the time of my youth prepared me for my time in the service.

After about eight months of living in St. Croix, I returned home to Statia feeling disappointed and feeling like a failure. I was plagued by questions. What did I do wrong? Why couldn't I stay and attend school as planned? Why did I have to come back?

The abrupt transition after finally venturing out on my own left me saddened for weeks. I replayed events in my head, wondering what more I could have done to change the outcome. But despite my best efforts, not everything had gone according to plan.

With time and reflection, I came to accept that some things are simply outside of our control. I realized that perceived setbacks are often blessings in disguise, opening new, unforeseen doors.

Though it took me a while to recognize it, this unexpected chapter closing marked the start of an important new beginning. I had to trust that my journey would unfold as it should.

When I returned to Statia, I attended what would become the Gwendoline van Putten (GVP) Technical School, the island's only secondary and vocational institution. They offered academic and hands-on classes in carpentry and masonry skills. This training paved the way for me to pursue a career in construction and cabinetry, work I understood from prior hands-on experience but lacked the proper skills and training to perform well.

In shop classes, I learned to use power tools and make items like window frames, doorframes, tables, and chairs as well as lay blocks and plaster walls and install tile.

GVP was about a 30-minute walk from home. Classes were small, around 8-10 students in a class, and there were three grade levels. The teachers were laid-back but expected you to complete assignments, which impacted your grades.

I was a solid B student, although I was often impatient for the school day to end so I could work and earn money.

Business drove me more than academics did. I worked construction helper jobs on weekends, holidays, and whenever classes ended early to gain experience. The skills from class later allowed me to design and build my first house at age 26.

I didn't play team sports or join any social clubs on the island. Working and making money felt addictively rewarding and perpetuated my desire to keep earning.

When I was fifteen, my older brothers moved to Statia and lived with us for a while, which was fun. We shared some chores, but it meant I also had to compete for my mom's attention. I loved hearing their relationship stories about their experiences with girls.

A highlight of my teenage social life was singing with friends in a band called SOS—Sons of the Soil. Some members of the popular roots band took us under their wings, teaching us to play various instruments and allowing us to perform as the openers at some of their gigs.

One year, I competed by performing solo in the Carnival Road March contest, taking the stage name Shot-A-Fire. I remixed a song by Calypso Rose. Although I didn't win, I still say I had the best Road March song that year—no doubt about it!

I admired icons like Mighty Sparrow and Calypso Rose from Trinidad and Tobago, King Short Shirt from Antigua and Barbuda, King Beau Beau and Singing Olivia from St.

Maarten, Yellowman, Gregory Isaac, and Bob Marley from Jamaica.

While all journeys have twists and turns, this formative period taught me that perceived setbacks often pave the way for growth. Returning home with dashed hopes quickly morphed into an opportunity for self-discovery.

My resourcefulness flourished while living solo abroad. Facing this abrupt transition built resilience in me to roll with life's changes. Though my educational plans had stalled, new pathways emerged to expand my skills and experience.

What first seemed like failure sparked the creativity and adaptability that served me well as an entrepreneur. Had everything gone smoothly, I may not have cultivated such grit for overcoming obstacles.

In the end, what I first perceived as a wrong turn would put me back on track to ultimately live life on my own terms.

Here are some questions:

1. Have you ever had to move or change schools as a child or teen? How did you adapt to the transition?

2. Was there a time you tried a new recipe and it totally failed? How did you salvage the situation?

3. Has a family member or friend ever inspired you to pursue something like a career goal? How so?

4. Do you have any childhood memories of trying to start a small business or make money on your own? What did you do?

5. If you quit or changed course on an educational path, what prompted your decision and how did it turn out? Do you have any regrets?

The Mentor

Meeting Uncle Bill

My fourth business idea tapped into my coastal island roots. At the age of 14, I spent my time collecting seashells on the beach with holes in them, stringing them onto colorful necklaces, and selling them to tourists for $10 each.

With plenty of raw material coming in with the tides every day, it required minimal investment up front. Yet it opened my eyes to the lucrative concept of supply and demand in entrepreneurship.

The *Polynesia* cruise ship visited our island weekly; I sold multiple necklaces to the sunburned vacationers, earning anywhere from $70 to sometimes more than $100 in one day.

The truth was that selling came naturally to me. It could have been my smiling, adorable face—or maybe the necklaces just sold themselves. Who knows?

It was during this time that a pivotal mentor entered my life. Uncle Bill was a 70-year-old radio repairman from upstate New York who retired on the island with his wife. His church had assigned him to establish their Baha'i faith ministry and spread their message.

Uncle Bill firmly believed business and life were inextricably intertwined, a concept he called "*the business of life,*" which, over time, changed how I saw both.

He became my trusted advisor and a role model to me, imparting enduring words of wisdom that still guide me today.

When visiting during what became our weekly meetings, Uncle Bill exuded optimism and spiritual purpose. He taught me that passion and service to others are the true foundations of success.

He encouraged me to evaluate opportunities, make sound decisions, take calculated risks, and learn from failures—my own and others'. With his gentle guidance and steering, I gained vision and clarity about using my entrepreneurial aspirations to uplift myself and others.

Uncle Bill helped me awaken my fullest potential by treating me like the disciplined man of purpose he knew I could become. His sage advice often came through storytelling over homemade lemonade at the kitchen table. The discussions we had and the insights I absorbed during those memorable afternoons influenced me deeply and inspired my personal and professional paths from that moment forward.

My island upbringing—intertwined with Uncle Bill's spiritual outlook—shaped my character and my outlook tremendously. From then on, as I went about my life, I strove to pay forward his mentoring by guiding youth, hoping to spark their potential as he did mine.

Uncle Bill showed me the power of heeding wisdom and accepting the generosity handed down from generation to generation.

While walking the beach collecting shells one afternoon, I met an older gentleman who introduced himself as Uncle Bill. Our conversation went something like this:

Uncle Bill: "Hello, young man! How are you doing today?"

Me: "Good afternoon, sir. I'm good."

Uncle Bill: "What are you up to?"

Me: "I'm picking up seashells."

Uncle Bill: "But I see you're keeping some and dropping others back onto the sand."

Me: "That's because I can only use the ones with natural holes. I string them up to make necklaces and sell them. Would you like to buy one?

Uncle Bill: "No, thank you, son. Have you ever tried making the holes yourself?"

Me: "Yes, but they often break when I try, so I just leave those on the beach."

Uncle Bill: "What would you like to be when you grow up?"

Me: "A businessman or manager."

Uncle Bill: "Well, you're already running a business! Let me ask you some questions. Are you still in school?"

Me: "Yes, sir."

Uncle Bill: "Who wakes you up each morning?"

Me: "I have an alarm clock to wake myself up."

Uncle Bill: "Do you have home chores?"

Me: "Yes, I do."

Uncle Bill: "How do you get to school?"

Me: "I walk there and back."

Uncle Bill: "Do teachers assign homework?"

Me: "Yes, they do."

Uncle Bill: "When do you complete your assignments?"

Me: "In between classes or in the evenings at home."

Uncle Bill: "You see, you're already a manager!"

Me: "Excuse me?"

Uncle Bill: "Young man, you are waking yourself up every morning, doing your morning chores, getting to and from school, getting homework assignments done, and making and selling seashell necklaces. You are already managing yourself. If you don't know how to manage yourself, no one will ever let you manage anything of theirs. You can be anything you want to be, and you're already a manager and a businessman."

I was stunned! It felt like light bulbs were switching on in my head. I was already running my own enterprise? No one had ever analyzed my daily habits and viewed me as a manager and a businessman before.

His perspective has stuck with me ever since. This was a pivotal moment in my life. Uncle Bill helped me recognize skills I didn't fully appreciate in myself.

Having someone see untapped potential in you at a young age is incredibly empowering. With the right drive, anyone can gain skills to reach their aspirations.

I went home and told my mom about Uncle Bill, the older man we often saw walking in our neighborhood. He had invited me to his home to review arts and crafts magazines so I could order supplies to expand my seashell jewelry business.

When I stopped by after school, I was amazed by all the options. With a small investment in tools like a drill press and supplies like necklace clasps and earring hooks, I could work much more efficiently. I could make three necklaces from the same material that normally made two by reducing the length. I could incorporate beads and other embellishments for more variety. Excited, I showed my mom the magazines and told her my ideas. Though initially hesitant, she gave her blessing.

I gave Uncle Bill $203—more than two weeks' worth of sales over two weeks' time, my largest investment ever—to order supplies from the magazines.

In 1983, before the internet and mobile phones were in use, mail order was like today's Amazon. The order forms were mailed to a U.S. company, then the items were shipped back to our island—a process that took between 9 and 12 weeks.

Unfortunately, Christmas came and went with no delivery, making the wait feel endless. But when my order finally arrived in January, it was like another Christmas, all for me! I received the tools and materials as promised.

This initial investment opened the doors to expand my business enterprise immensely. With my new drill press and supplies, I made diverse jewelry—shell bracelets and earrings for tourists and beaded necklaces and bracelets for friends and schoolmates.

I seized every selling opportunity that came my way on our small island. If I saw you and we said hello to each other, I would try to sell you something.

With Uncle Bill's mentorship, my entrepreneurial path came into focus. He gave me inspiration, resources, and confidence, assuring me that I would succeed.

His emotional and personal investment in me gave me assets of immense value that no youth can buy—knowledge, self-belief, and vision.

Transforming passion into purpose at a young age is a powerful force. Mentors like Uncle Bill have an immense impact by nurturing potential at a pivotal time. I'll always be grateful to him for helping me unlock my talents and opening the doors to my future.

These formative experiences instilled core business concepts within me, such as having the ability to spot opportunities, take calculated risks, make strategic investments, and execute ideas. The foundation built on those business principles during my youth still drives me today.

With encouragement and support, we can equip youth to unlock their potential as tomorrow's innovators and leaders. By investing our time, guidance, and resources in their growth, we can ignite that entrepreneurial spark.

Here are some insights on cultivating an entrepreneurial mindset in young people:

1. Entrepreneurship starts with creativity and vision—imagining the possibilities are endless.

2. Ideas arise from identifying issues and brainstorming solutions.

3. Actions require drive, taking calculated risks, and persistence.

4. Iterations refine feedback until a viable model emerges.

5. Self-doubt, fear of failure, and limited resources hinder progress.

With the right kind of encouragement—to think big, start small, and keep improving—young entrepreneurs can bring their visions to life.

Every one of us has untapped potential waiting to be unlocked with proper support.

Here are some questions:
1. Did you have someone in your youth who took an interest in mentoring you or nurturing your talents? What impact did they have?

2. What core values or pieces of wisdom were imparted to you by your role models when you were young?

3. Have you ever had an experience where someone recognized your potential before you saw it in yourself? How did that affect you?

4. Do you try to mentor or inspire youth today by seeing their untapped talents? Why is that important?

5. If you could instill one key belief or piece of advice in a child to set them up for success, what would it be?

The Time

Learning About Punctuality

One day, I arrived at Uncle Bill's house at 3:17 p.m. for our 3:00 meeting to learn bead-stringing techniques. On Statia, that was considered early because island residents often showed up 30 minutes late or more. We called this "Statia time."

I was greeted warmly by Aunty Margie, Uncle Bill's wife. "Come in, son, have a seat! Would you like some water, tea, or I have brown sugar lemonade, just like you make at home?"

The first time I had Aunty Margie's "lemonade," it tasted strange. She'd offered me a glass of homemade lemonade made with limes picked from the tree in their yard. I accepted and took a big gulp, but the flavor wasn't right—this was definitely not like our Statia homemade lemonade!

Aunty Margie and I exchanged confused looks at the same time.

Aunty Margie: "Do you like it? It's lemonade."

Me: "This is what you call lemonade? What kind is it?"

Aunty Margie: "Come see." We stepped over to the counter. "It's just lime juice, sugar, and water over ice," she explained.

Me: "At home, we make lemonade with brown sugar, not white."

So, I opted for a glass of lemonade and started drinking slowly—small gulp, small gulp—and then put my head back, and down it went.

She gave me half a smile and asked, "Did you like it?"

Me: "Yes! Yes, ma'am. The lemonade tastes good, thank you. Can I have another glass, please?"

Aunty Margie: "Yes, you can, son. Have a seat. Uncle Bill will be right in."

Sitting at the kitchen table, I sipped my second glass of lemonade as Uncle Bill joined me minutes later. Aunty Margie served him a glass of lemonade too.

Uncle Bill: "How are you doing, son?"

Me: "I'm doing fine, sir."

Uncle Bill took a sip and said, "I love brown sugar lemonade."

Uncle Bill: "How was school today?"

Me: "School was fine, sir."

Uncle Bill: "How many classes did you have today?"

Me: "Three classes."

Uncle Bill: "Did you get to all your classes on time?"

Me: "Yes, I did. I'm never late for class."

Uncle Bill: "What time did your last class end?"

Me: "It ended at 2 o'clock."

Uncle Bill: "We had an agreement that we would meet here at 3 o'clock but you were 20 minutes late. How is it that you can get to three classes on time in one day, yet you arrived 20 minutes late to our meeting?"

I apologized for losing track of time.

Uncle Bill: "Unfortunately, since you didn't arrive at 3 p.m. as expected, I made other plans, and we'll have to reschedule."

I asked if we could meet on Thursday instead. Uncle Bill agreed but warned me that if I was late again, he wouldn't meet with me anymore.

He explained that lateness shows disrespect and dishonesty. By his way of thinking, we had an agreement, which I broke, along with my word. "If you can be on time for one thing, you can be on time for everything," he remarked.

I left feeling disappointed in myself but committed to never being late for Uncle Bill again. Looking back, this meeting marked an early lesson in the stark contrast between laid-back "Statia time" and Uncle Bill's strict punctuality.

While island life moved at a relaxed pace, Uncle Bill taught me that respecting others' time fosters trust—a valuable insight that paved the way for success in my future relationships.

Moving forward, I integrated both cultural approaches in my life. For business affairs, I adopted Uncle Bill's focus on timeliness, recognizing it as key to gaining credibility. But during social occasions, I retained some flexibility, inspired by Statia's casual "island time."

Balancing structure with leisure, I found the perfect rhythm to thrive across cultures. Though a tough lesson that day, Uncle Bill's wisdom about punctuality stuck with me and served me well in the *business of life.*

Questions to consider:

1. Why are you sometimes late?

2. Do you prioritize punctuality?

3. How does lateness impact others?

4. What can you do to improve?

5. Are you willing to commit to discipline and planning ahead?

Here are some more questions:

1. Were values like punctuality and respect for others' time instilled in you from a young age? What shaped that?

2. Do you recall any pivotal moments growing up when being late led to meaningful consequences or lessons?

3. In what ways were you motivated as a kid to be accountable and keep your word when making agreements?

4. What benefits have you experienced in your adult life from being punctual and respectful of others' time?

5. As a parent, how do you try to instill strong values like punctuality, respect, accountability, and integrity in your kids?

The Five-Year Plan

Mapping Out the Future

One day, Uncle Bill asked me, "Where do you see yourself in the next five years?" This wasn't something I had thought much about at the age of 15.

He explained that he had been making 5-year plans ever since he turned 20. While they didn't always go exactly as planned, he generally came close to achieving his goals and sometimes even exceeded his expectations.

He taught me that "Failing to plan is a plan to fail."

"Come on, son, think about it. Shake that thing inside your head," he said. "Let's break it down one year at a time."

I started thinking while sipping some lemonade and then responded, "Okay, I've got some ideas."

For years one and two, I planned to continue working and selling my products, save money, and finish school.

In year three, I hoped to get a good job, find a girlfriend, and keep saving money.

For year four, my goal was to buy a piece of land and continue saving.

In year five, I wanted to get married, start building a house, and live happily ever after.

Uncle Bill said, "See, son, that wasn't so difficult. Now you have specific targets to work toward each year for the next five years. Five years from today, you'll look back on this conversation and evaluate if you met or exceeded your expectations."

He assured me it was okay if things didn't go exactly according to plan. The plan provided a benchmark for comparison. But changing the plan to suit an ever-evolving reality is like moving the goalposts down the field in order to score—that doesn't happen. If you can't quite make it to the goal, you have to keep pushing forward and maybe pass the ball."

In my mind, my next five years would be an adventure guided by lessons learned and experiences derived from the past. *I'm going to take the ball and run with it,* I thought, *and then I'll pass the ball, shifting my position as needed. Then I'll get the ball back and score. "Gooooooooooal!"*

Well, here is how my next five years actually played out:

- Year 1: I continued working, selling my products, saving, and going to school as planned.

- Year 2: I quit school, worked briefly in a kitchen, a retail store, and construction, then migrated to St. Maarten and found work as a carpenter building decks and patios.

- Year 3: I got a girlfriend, we broke up, and she broke my heart. I moved and changed jobs.

- Year 4: I found a new girlfriend, worked two jobs, and went to Casino School.

- Year 5: I got a job at one casino and then switched to another. I moved to the French side of the island, bought my first car, and became engaged.

While my meticulous Five-Year Plan quickly veered off course, its value lay in envisioning possibilities and setting ambitious goals. Though life often charted its own route, the exercise expanded my perspective and planted seeds of aspiration.

Dreaming big at Uncle Bill's urging motivated my drive and tenacity to achieve, even if specific paths diverged. More than the plan itself, his mentoring instilled the vision, self-belief, and burning desire critical for entrepreneurial success.

Rather than rigidly sticking to a prescribed road map, the flexibility to adapt became my secret weapon. As long as the passion Uncle Bill ignited continued propelling me forward, the unfolding journey brought valuable lessons and experiences.

Though not always smooth, my circuitous entrepreneurial route built character and resilience that guides me to this day.

Here are some questions:

1. Did you ever create 5 or 10-year plans for your life when you were younger? How did they evolve?

2. Looking back, what core goals have you maintained throughout your life so far? What has changed?

3. What experiences shaped your goals and vision for the future when you were a teen?

4. How did key mentors influence the way you thought about mapping out your plans and dreams?

5. If you guided a young person today, what wisdom would you share about long-term goal-setting and handling detours?

Bullying

Difficult Experiences with Bullying

I remember being in fifth grade when I had my first run-in with the police. I was scared, crying, and was locked in a jail cell.

It seems that bullies have existed for as long as humanity. Growing up, it was hard to avoid the troublemakers. They didn't take my lunch money or give me wedgies, but they were annoying people who targeted anyone they thought was weak or couldn't fight back.

The term "St. Kitts nigger" was, and still is, commonly used to refer to Kittitians. This was not considered hate speech or discrimination by most at that time. However, as a young black boy from St. Kitts, I understood it as a derogatory racial slur from learning about slavery and segregation in my American history class.

I would sometimes get angry when referred to by racial slurs or when facing prejudicial treatment. Despite having friends, I rarely felt we were equals; I often felt like an outsider in my own community.

I coped by pouring my energy into my work, driven by a passion and desire to succeed.

I never saw any point in fighting, so I would always walk away from aggressive or confrontational people. Fighting with one person would mean I might have to fight with their brothers, sisters, cousins, or even their best friend another day.

If a bully wanted to fight me after school, they were going to have to catch me first! When the last bell rang, I was the first one out of the gate, turning my 15-minute walk home into a five-minute dash.

That morning was a tipping point in my life. The beast within me was about to get out of its cage. Here is what happened that landed me in a jail cell.

One day, some of my classmates wadded some paper into a ball and were tossing it around when the teacher wasn't looking. Suddenly, one of them threw it, hitting the teacher squarely in the back. It made a loud "thwack" and then fell to the floor.

When he turned around, they all immediately pointed at me and said in unison, "He did it!" I tried to protest and tell the teacher I wasn't involved in their mischief and didn't see who threw it. My indignation, however, was met with an icy glare and stony silence.

My undeserved punishment was to stay behind in the classroom during morning recess for supposedly disrupting the rest of the class. I also had to write on every line of two full pages from my notebook: "I am sorry for disrupting class and hitting the teacher."

I was really angry and felt helpless. The teacher did not care about my side. He did not even listen to me.

During recess, however, while I was writing my lines, one of the instigators snuck back into the classroom to tease me and shove me around while the others stood guard at the door. I warned him to leave me alone, but he just continued taunting me.

With the door closed behind him, neither one of us was prepared for what would happen next.

With him pushing me back against the wall, I head-butted him in the face, causing his nose to bleed, and stabbed him with the pen I had in my hand—first in the left shoulder, then again on the right shoulder from behind as he turned.

Screaming, he rushed to the door. I went back to my desk and picked up my pencil, anticipating others coming into the classroom for me. I had to be ready to defend myself if needed.

But when the door remained shut, I took a deep breath to calm down. Rage had gotten the better of me. It took me a minute to realize what I had done in retaliation and what I was prepared to do if they came back.

I had made another kid bleed.

Two teachers came inside the classroom and told me to just sit down at my desk and relax. About five minutes after the bell rang, recess was over, but none of my classmates came into my classroom after the incident.

One teacher left the class and closed the door as they went. Moments later, there was a knock on the door. When the teacher opened it, there was a police officer.

I didn't know what was happening. What have I done? I started crying, thinking it wasn't my fault. I had not meant for that to happen. I honestly hadn't intended to hurt my classmate; I just wanted him to stop harassing me. But in my anger, I had lost control.

The police officer held my hand and walked me out. On the way out of the class, there was complete silence. My entire class just stood outside watching us leave.

I was crying, with my head down all the way to the police car. The officer asked, "Do you know what happens to bad boys?" Crying, I said, "But I'm not a bad boy."

But apparently, he thought I was because just like on television, the bad guy ends up in the back of a police car headed to jail, which was now my fate.

We got to the police station, and I was placed in a cell and locked up for about 30 minutes before being taken to a room with a table and three chairs. There, I recounted to the officer exactly what had happened. He left and returned with a notepad and pen, asking me to write down my statement.

After I finished documenting the incident as well as I could, he left again. The next time he came back, he brought me a cheese sandwich and a soda. I promised the officer I would never get in trouble again. We shook on it to seal the promise.

I was petrified, sitting there wondering what was happening. I wanted my mom. I wanted to go home. Time seemed frozen for an eternity.

But by the day's end, the officer informed me that they had spoken to my classmate and his dad, and my classmate had admitted to instigating the trouble. The officer then said, "I'm taking you home now."

That's when I really started to panic! This wasn't just a teacher's note or someone complaining about me. I had not gone home for lunch or arrived by 3:15 p.m. as usual.

Instead, I was getting dropped off at the end of the day by the police!

My mind began to race, picturing my mom sitting on the porch waiting with a belt across her lap. I was returning home in a police car—her worst nightmare.

Then I thought, she must have been worried sick wondering where I was. Of course, there was no way she didn't know what had happened.

I wished with all my might that the earth would open up and swallow me whole before we got there. In fact, I was so scared that I asked the officer if I could go home with him instead. He chuckled, then assured me, "Don't worry, we already spoke to your mother, and she understands what happened."

As we turned down my street, I slunk down in the back seat, trying to become invisible. But the car soon pulled up to my house. My mom was indeed sitting outside, stone-faced. The neighbors stood gawking nearby. There was no escaping now. I took a deep breath and braced myself as the officer opened the door. Judgment Day had arrived.

To my surprise, when I got home, my mom hugged me and we went inside. I was imagining she'd be waiting there for me with a belt, ready to unleash her fury.

But after the initial shock, she was compassionate. I washed up, ate dinner, showered, and went straight to bed. I cried myself to sleep that night, replaying the day's traumatic events. It was one of the longest days of my life.

When I returned to school days later, my classmates and I shook hands and apologized to each other, and that was the end of it.

But four years later, I found myself back in that exact same office, sitting on the same side of the table with that same police officer, apologizing for breaking my promise.

Only this time, I spent a long weekend locked in a cell. I was lonely, having conversations with myself: *I don't belong here. This shouldn't have happened. We were friends, and our parents were friends.*

It was a life-changing experience—one I solemnly vowed never to repeat. Here's how it happened.

We were doing a three-day masonry project in my second year at GVP.

Day 1: Build a connecting blocked wall.

Day 2: Plaster both sides of the wall.

Day 3: Place tiles on one side of the wall.

Some of my classmates were horsing around, throwing chips from the blocks and stones at others. Some of them came my way.

I ignored it at first, but it didn't stop. I started getting angry, and I warned them to keep me out of it, that I wasn't part of their game.

I was already upset because I was having issues placing some tiles. Then on top of that, I had to deal with stones and blocks being thrown at me. I took about a third of a block to rest against a tile to keep it in place because it kept sliding from its place. I stood up, and a piece of rock came and hit me in the head. I had seen my friend and classmate, hand in motion, throwing it. In my rage, I picked up the piece of block and threw it back at my friend, hitting him across the face. He fell to the ground. I picked up my hammer in hand, ready to defend myself in case he decided to come at me.

I was ready to charge forward to stop him if he tried to retaliate. I was like a caged animal that had just gotten loose.

I heard a teacher call out, "Hey, stop!" In that second, I stood still and took a breath. It was over. Or was it? My friend was on the ground as the teacher rushed over to see what was wrong with him.

He stood up and was taken to the classroom, where a wet rag was placed on the side of his face.

I left school and began walking home. I'm not sure who called the police, but on my way home, a police car pulled up next to me and told me to get in.

I was in trouble—once again finding myself in the back of a police car. This was the worst feeling.

I replayed the events over and over in my mind, convinced that I was not the bad guy here.

The officer took me to the station and put me in a cell. This time, I was strip-searched and had to remove my shoelaces.

I sat on the bunk bed for more than an hour before being taken out of the cell and shown to the same office where I had been four years earlier.

But it seemed like I was facing some serious trouble now. Two officers came into the room this time—the one I had made a promise to four years before, along with another officer.

I was scared. The officer said to me, "Browne, we meet again. You promised me you would stay out of trouble. Why do we need to meet in this room again?"

Crying with my head down and staring at the floor, I apologized for breaking my promise from four years earlier.

He said I was no longer a little 12-year-old boy; I was a 16-year-old, and boys my age, they said, don't get to go home at the end of the day; they spend a long, long time in jail.

"Do you want to go to jail?"

I was crying, "No, no, I don't want to go to jail; it wasn't my fault. I didn't do anything wrong. I was just defending myself. The other guy should go to jail for hitting me with a rock in my head. He's the troublemaker, not me."

The other officer just stood there quietly, not saying anything. He was just looking at me as if he understood. Then he left the room and came back about two minutes later with a sandwich and a Coke and told me to eat. They both left the room.

After 20 minutes, the other officer came back into the room and brought a notepad and pen. He told me to write down what had happened and to let him know when I was finished.

As soon as I was done, I called out to him. Both policemen came into the room, took the pad, and read what I had written down.

The new officer said, "Okay, Browne. Come on, I'll put you back in the cell. You'll be sleeping here tonight."

I started crying again. Yes, I was in real trouble this time.

I asked him, "Can't you help me?"

He said, "No, this is what happens when you hit your classmate with a piece of block. You go to jail, boy!"

I was locked up from Thursday afternoon until Monday morning. There was no one else there except a guard and the mosquitoes.

I was given a breakfast sandwich around 8 a.m. and a dinner sandwich around 5 p.m. The main meal was just after noon.

After the first night, I took a shower the next day and changed into other clothes they had picked up from my mom.

The weekend stay was mentally draining; I was just there locked in a cell like the caged chickens in our backyard. Except I had no other chickens around me to talk to.

The guard told me to call out if I needed anything. I asked him if he could let me go home and sleep, promising to come back early the next day before anyone found out. He told me to just relax and get some sleep, and tomorrow would be better.

It seemed to me that jail was a complete waste of my valuable time. Somehow, the minutes and hours seemed to slow to a crawl in jail.

By Monday morning, the police officers came in and asked me how I was doing. I said I just wanted to go home.

The police told me they had spoken to my classmate and his mother. My classmate admitted to instigating the trouble that led to me throwing the block.

No formal complaint was filed, so I could go home.

Yet the uncertainty plagued my mind in the days after the ordeal. I kept wondering, *Was this really over? Would there be a revenge plot by my classmate, his brothers, or his friends? Would I end up in another fight or be locked up again?*

I wanted to leave the island to escape the lingering fears of retaliation that lurked in my head. No one likes losing a fight, even when they start it.

My mother and I did not discuss the bullying incident in great detail. She simply said that she and her friend, the mother of my classmate, would talk it over. I should not talk with anyone about it.

A few days later, I worked up the courage to go to their home and apologize face to face for what I had done, even though he had provoked me. My classmate's mother graciously accepted my apology on his behalf.

I chose not to speak about the situation anymore after that. I wanted to put the ugly incident behind me and continue moving forward. But the desire to leave our small island grew stronger, fueled by my restless hopes of somehow starting anew.

Then about six weeks after the incident with the block, the best friend of my former friend who I'd hit in the head blindsided me and hit me in the head with a hammer in the middle of the school day.

I saw stars instantly. I held my head and could feel something warm and wet. I looked at my hand—yes, I was bleeding.

I was angry and worried at the same time. I heard other classmates saying, "He's bleeding, he's bleeding. Boy, you're in trouble!" This was clearly a retaliation strike orchestrated by his best friend. The teacher found a rag, and I held it to my head to stop the bleeding.

When it finally subsided, I got a bandage and went to the hospital. I believe my anger was blocking out the pain. The doctor put three stitches in my head, which really hurt. Then I went home.

The police came to our house and said they had apprehended the boy who assaulted me with the hammer. The police took my statement and said they would handle it from there.

The very scenario I had feared came to pass, catching me completely off guard. This boy had a history of troublemaking and had been locked up before. He was locked up for about two weeks for this attack, then released.

I don't think my mother knew how to handle this situation. I thought there could be more surprise attacks and was afraid I would have to constantly look over my shoulder.

For the first time, I believed I had enemies who could strike at any time, and I worried that I'd never be free of this threat.

Growing up, I'd watched my stepdad sharpen his machete when preparing to slaughter a goat or sheep. Now I did the same with my machete and a knife. I carried the knife in my school bag and hid the machete at school. I could have died that day from the blow to my head.

I was angry, hurt, and alone. With my brothers having left the island for St. Kitts, and no father in sight, I felt completely vulnerable. I prayed and asked God to give me courage and strength and to calm my fears.

Even so, I retreated into myself, gripped by anger, worry, and desperation all at once. I refused to stand by waiting for another attack. I was convinced I needed to strike first to protect myself from further harm.

My mind raced as I touched the bandage covering my wound. Three stitches held together the gash from that sneak hammer attack.

It was a simple yet impossible choice—live out my days in jail or potentially die there at school.

The next day, the teacher informed us that the boy had been expelled from school and would not be coming back after his release. In my rage and desperation, I considered taking matters into my own hands, heedless of the consequences.

Though this offered some comfort, I took my machete home but remained on high alert, keeping the knife close by in my bag. The lingering fear of retaliation stayed with me in the uneasy days that followed.

The next time I met with Uncle Bill, we talked about what had happened and how I was feeling about it. He told me I needed to:

- Start controlling my surroundings better, like where I placed myself and with whom I became friends.
- Avoid loud, aggressive, mischievous, and plain old stupid people.
- Learn to walk away from friends who are mean to others, even if they're nice to me.
- Focus my efforts more on myself, become driven to learn, and work hard to increase my chances of success.

- Realize that where I come from does not determine where I end up.
- Know that if I forget where I come from, I'll be lost and never find the direction I want to go in.
- Understand that my past has brought me to where I am in the present. I must own my current circumstances while I plan my future.
- Learn to understand another person's point of view, though I could agree to disagree and walk away.
- Consider that the two places with the most unfulfilled dreams and immense talents are cemeteries and prisons—but prisons are avoidable.
- Remember that all of my eggs are in one basket, and that basket is me.

His words penetrated my anger, giving me pause.

I resolved to find another way, refusing to let the attackers make me the villain. I stared at my reflection, realizing the grim outcome violence could bring. I could have been that 16-year-old kid who caused so much pain for so many.

Though shaken, I emerged on the other side of darkness with my spirit intact. Hardened but not embittered, I forgave but did not forget.

I wanted to quit school. I wanted to leave Statia, but I had questions. Was I ready for the world? Where would I go? When would I leave? What would I do when I got there? I had to come up with answers, but at that moment, I had none.

While intensely painful, these formative bullying experiences taught me to transcend negativity by responding, not reacting.

Though we can't control others, we can control our response. The power lies in how we react. I learned to disengage from unnecessary conflicts and not internalize others' issues.

Rather than being consumed by the experience, I channeled the energy into bettering myself. Through self-discipline, I avoided wasting time on petty disputes or retaliation.

Staying focused on my goals kept me on a positive track, not derailed by distractions.

Hardships build resilience and character. By managing my surroundings and relationships proactively, I curated an environment conducive to growth.

Eliminating toxic influences opened doors for mentorship to thrive. With maturity comes understanding different perspectives.

Rising above challenges ultimately empowers you. Progress depends on converting stumbling blocks into stepping stones toward your aspirations. With the right mindset, each experience, whether positive or negative, provides an opportunity to learn and grow.

Remember, you have a choice. You can let anger take over, or you can find another way.

Look inside to the love in your heart. I know it's there, even when it might be hard to see. Absorb this truth: love is stronger than any anger.

Take a breath and let it fill you up. Feel it soothing the rage and calming the storm within. You have the power to overcome this. Don't let the anger win.

Hard-won wisdom equips us to handle adversity and come out stronger. By keeping my eyes on the horizon, I didn't lose sight of my greater dreams and purpose.

Here are some questions:

1. When faced with adversity like bullying, how did you find the strength to persevere and not let it defeat you? What lessons did it teach you?

2. Have you transformed negative experiences into positives that ultimately helped you grow? What did that look like?

3. What self-discipline strategies help you avoid wasting energy on toxic people or petty disputes? How do you stay focused?

4. How have you cultivated relationships and an environment that brings out your best self? What changes did you make?

5. When have you channeled anger or hardship into personal betterment rather than retaliation? What drives that mindset shift?

Cost of Living

Budgeting and Money Lessons

When I asked Uncle Bill a question, I'd sometimes get more questions in return or a story as the answer.

One day, I told Uncle Bill I was ready to leave the island behind and never come back. I was convinced that life was too short to wait until I got older—I needed his help now. He responded, "Sure, son," then got up and went into the living room.

I think the delay tactic was his way of gathering his thoughts to address my overactive teenage mind. Aunty Margie came in and refilled our lemonade glasses. Uncle Bill sat back down; class was in session.

"First of all, son, life is only short for those taking shortcuts," Uncle Bill said. "A shortcut may get you to a destination faster. But in life, the final destination is death, so there's no need to rush toward it. Don't take shortcuts. I'm 72 years old with more years behind me than ahead. Do you comprehend how old 72 years is? Do you realize how long it takes to reach 72 years of age? Life is not a race to cross the finish line first. It's a journey you start, hoping to be the last one to finish. You could live long enough to add my 72 years to your 16 years, but I may not survive that long. So, never call life short; it's the longest state of consciousness we know. Do you understand what I'm saying?"

"Yes, sir," I replied.

He continued, "So, you want to leave Statia forever? Let me ask you some questions then:

"Where do you want to go?"

"When will you leave?"

"Where will you live?

"How will you support yourself?"

"How much do you think living alone costs?"

"Have you discussed this with your parents?"

"Being tall doesn't make you a man. You're not an adult yet. You can't just go live alone before you're 18. I need answers if I'm to help you."

I put the glass to my mouth and drained it, pondering his questions, to which I had no real answers.

Uncle Bill looked at me and said, "If you can answer me, maybe I can help you."

Needing answers but having none, I stared at my empty glass, wishing for more lemonade.

He said, "Come on, son, shake that thing inside your head."

I said, "Well, I have money in my bank account."

He said, "Okay, how much?"

"5,127 guilders," I said.

"Do you know how much it costs to live alone?" he questioned.

"No, sir," I said.

Uncle Bill got up, went to the living room, and returned with a pencil and paper. "The moment you leave your parents' home, all bills and living expenses become yours. You will have to spend money on more than just personal items. You'll have monthly expenses to pay forever. Write this down: rent, electricity, food, and laundry, to start."

Uncle Bill: "How much is rent?"

Me: "About 300 guilders."

Uncle Bill: "Electricity?"

Me: "About 30 guilders."

Uncle Bill: "Food?"

Me: "I don't know."

Uncle Bill: "Let's say 25 guilders a day."

Uncle Bill: "Laundry?"

Me: "About 10 guilders weekly."

Uncle Bill: "Okay, mister businessman, total your monthly costs."

Me (calculating): "1,120 guilders."

Uncle Bill: "What's your monthly income?"

Me: "I don't know."

Uncle Bill: "You'll need at least 1,120 guilders a month excluding entertainment, clothes, et cetera. And your own place needs a fridge, stove, bed, washer, sheets, pots, plates, and cleaning supplies. Do you know their costs?"

Me: "No."

Uncle Bill: "What's your cost of living at home?"

Me: "Nothing."

Uncle Bill: "Sounds like a good deal. You should stay for as long as you can, finish school, work, and save until you can afford to go. Don't you agree?"

Me: "Yes, sir! May I have more lemonade, please?"

Uncle Bill poured me another glass—and then class continued.

"Living with your parents is free. The moment you leave, you'll need to budget. No matter where you go or where you live, you will have monthly expenses for the rest of your life.

You also need to be sure they're less than the money you earn."

"Open your school bag and take out your math textbook and a ruler. I'll teach you how to make a cost-of-living budget," Uncle Bill said.

Following Uncle Bill's instructions, I turned to a blank page in the back of my math book and drew four columns. At the top of each column, I wrote the headings: income and description in the first two columns, then expenses and description in the last two.

He explained that every month I should list all money earned under income and briefly describe where it came from under "description." Then under "expenses," I should record everything spent and write what it was for under "description." Then I needed to total each column and subtract the expenses total from the income total.

Uncle Bill advised me to save at least half of whatever was left over, just in case I got sick and couldn't work or lost my job. This budgeting methodology provided the framework to track my finances and build up my savings.

A basic personal savings plan is to save at least three months of your monthly expenses yearly.

Uncle Bill strongly encouraged me to establish my banking habits, saying it was wise to open a bank account to deposit savings wherever I lived. Having an account establishes a financial identity with the bank.

Plus, it builds a profile of you as a saver over time. Then when you need a loan for business or personal reasons, the bank can easily review your history of making frequent deposits. This demonstrates to them that you are capable of repaying borrowed money.

Starting early with disciplined savings habits shows banks that you handle finances responsibly—making you a trustworthy future borrower.

As the saying goes: "Chance favors the prepared." Build a strong banking relationship before you need a loan. This will give you access to capital if the time comes when you require it.

Learning and adopting this money management lesson at a young age paved the way to grow businesses in my adulthood. From that day on, the insights were mine to keep forever. I felt ready to take on the world armed with my newfound knowledge.

Decades later, the budgeting methodologies I learned back then still stick with me. I have been using these principles to guide my finances ever since.

While budgeting may seem tangential to entrepreneurship, the financial planning skills I learned from Uncle Bill provided the foundation for making smart choices managing money and assessing risk when launching my businesses. By understanding how to track income and expenses, I was able to make informed financial decisions.

I gained critical skills in cost projection, budget discipline, and separating needs versus wants. As an entrepreneur with limited resources, these budgeting fundamentals allowed me to maximize my capital, minimize unnecessary costs, and set savings goals.

My mentor imparted core financial literacy principles when I was still at a young age, which served me well in assessing risks and opportunities throughout my business ventures.

Although impatient in my youth, Uncle Bill's wisdom about avoiding shortcuts and not rushing through life stuck with me over the years. He taught me that great rewards come to those who wait, plan properly, and put in the hard work.

This lesson proved invaluable when launching my businesses later on. Resisting shortcuts built strong foundations that withstood the tests of time. I learned that patience and dedication compound into lasting success.

Of course, Uncle Bill and I didn't always see eye to eye. My impatient, impulsive teenage mind often butted heads with his measured, methodical approach. Yet he handled our clashes of perspective with patience and understanding.

Over time, I came to appreciate Uncle Bill's outlook more as my focus shifted from immediate gratification to building things of enduring value. He showed me how small daily steps made with purpose can culminate in giant leaps over a lifetime. His insights guided me to create things meant to last and not to just chase instant rewards.

Here are some questions:

1. What money management skills did key mentors or family members pass on to you when you were young?

2. Do you recall any pivotal moments in your youth where you gained important financial literacy? What core money values or savings habits were instilled in you early on?

3. How did childhood lessons shape your attitudes and behaviors concerning budgets, expenses, and saving versus spending?

4. What money skills or mindsets would you strive to impart to guide a young person now and set them up for success in the future?

5. What parallels exist between budgeting your household and budgeting a startup venture? How might mastering personal budgeting and money management skills at a young age equip someone to handle business finances and strategically take action?

Goodbye and Hello

Leaving Home and Returning

Uncle Bill told me the five ways a person can increase their chances of living a productive and success-filled life. They were:

1. Finish high school and go to college, graduate, start a career, work your way to the top of your field, make and save money, live a good life, and retire well.

2. Finish high school and join a government service like law enforcement, the military, fire rescue, health care, education, etc. Work your way up the ranks, save money, live a good life, and retire well with a good pension.

3. Finish high school and, if you're an athlete, pray you don't get a severe injury early on that ends your career. Also, save your money, live a good life, and retire well.

4. Finish high school, learn a skill or a trade through a vocational or apprenticeship program, follow a career, save your money, live a good life, and retire well.

5. Finish high school, go out into the world, and learn to do as many different jobs as you can. Then between the one that you love and the one you do

best, use them both and create a business that can pay your way through life. Finally, save money, live a good life, and retire well.

At the end of my second year at GVP, I decided it was time to quit school. I was determined, driven, and confident I could do it on my own. Statia felt like a small pond, and I wanted to venture out into the open ocean.

I spoke to my mom about not returning for my final year because I no longer had an interest in continuing my schooling. I promised her that I would get a job instead to help her financially and also save money myself. She responded that if I wasn't going to school, I needed to get a job or I couldn't continue living in her house. She had no idea that my ultimate plan was to work and save up enough money to leave Statia for good.

I was eager to get out into the real world and prove myself. Statia was a small, close-knit community, and I dreamed of bigger things.

Although school had provided a solid structure and platform from which to launch, I felt ready to take charge of life on my own terms. I knew the five life systems would guide me in living productively and finding success.

With fierce determination, I set my sights on independence.

Yes, I was ready. I was all in. I wanted to increase my chances to live a good life and retire well. I quit school and started working at a restaurant making burgers on the grill, fries, shakes, and other sandwiches, then I worked in a retail clothing store, and later, I went to work in construction, all in the first year after leaving school.

Uncle Bill did not approve of my decision to quit school, but he said the choice was mine to make. He told me that the ability to think for ourselves and choose our own paths is part of what makes us human. Learning through past mistakes and applying those lessons is a superpower. He cautioned me to learn from the mistakes of others as well as my own, to help me grow.

"No man is an island" is a popular island phrase. It means we need one another—we are our community. He urged me to create a resource circle using anything and anyone who could help me reach my goals and dreams. And that I too must become a resource to my circle by sharing my knowledge.

Uncle Bill warned me not to expect any handouts in the world. Life isn't fair. To achieve what I want, I'll likely need to be twice as smart, work twice as hard, and wait twice as long as expected to see my dreams realized. But I can't give up; I must keep pushing forward.

His advice was to stay strong, focused, and believe in myself. Understand that the life experiences I gain will come at the cost of innocence, with maturity as my reward.

As I move up in the world, I'll need to adapt my thinking and behavior—what I'm used to won't apply everywhere and to everyone. When times get tough, I should pause, take a deep breath, and reflect wisely.

Sometimes after talking to Uncle Bill, I walked away feeling heavy, as if 10 pounds of wisdom was just deposited in my head. That priceless guidance was now mine to keep, locked in my mind forever. What would I do with it? I had to use it. But how?

I was still making seashells and bead products and selling them. I made time to meet with Uncle Bill, arriving 15 to 20 minutes early. Aunty Margie would tell me all about her garden, crocheting and knitting, and how much she loved brown sugar lemonade while I waited for Uncle Bill to come.

Uncle Bill and I talked about going to the island of St. Maarten. He said I would have more opportunities there to sell my products because of the high volume of tourists compared to Statia. Through his Baha'i faith connections, he arranged for me to stay in St. Maarten for two weeks.

I was 17 when I left Statia, headed to St. Maarten with the intent of staying for those two weeks. I thought if it went well, I'd return to Statia, empty my bank account, fly back to St. Maarten, and start a new life.

I saved all the money from the last weeks of sales to invest in my St. Maarten trip. I also made lots of extra items to sell, increasing my inventory for the weeks ahead. This was my moment of truth—the moment I'd been waiting for—a chance to prove myself.

The plan was sound and I was as prepared as I could be. I had a duffel bag stuffed full of my most vibrant shell necklaces and beaded bracelets. I had seeds, shells, and beaded earrings. I had enough savings for a meal for several weeks while getting my budding business established.

At the airport before boarding, I looked up at the dormant volcanic peaks of The Quill with deep affection and said, "Goodbye, Statia. I'll be back."

The distance between St. Maarten and Statia is only about 65 miles (105 km) as the seagull flies. The two islands are close neighbors, with Statia lying northwest of St. Maarten, a quick 17-minute flight away.

Nestled in the eastern Caribbean around 150 miles east of Puerto Rico lies the small island of St. Maarten, nicknamed "Sunshine City" and "the Friendly Island." Split between the Dutch and French, it's a tiny landmass at just 37 square miles, making it the smallest island divided between two countries. Lining its shores are 365 beaches, so beachgoers can enjoy a different stretch of sand every day.

St. Maarten boasts a cultural blend of Dutch, French, English, and Spanish influences. Duty-free shopping abounds, offering deals on jewelry, liquor, tobacco, and electronics.

Beyond the beaches, hiking the rolling hills is a real treasure. There, you'll find Fort Amsterdam, a 17th-century fortress standing watch over the island.

As St. Maarten peeked into view from the plane window, the endless possibilities swirled in my mind. I was determined to throw myself fully into this venture. This was my chance to pave my own path. If passion, belief in my abilities and some seeds of capital could make it happen, then I was sure my enterprise would thrive even in unfamiliar terrain.

Sunshine City called my name. The time had come to sink or swim, chasing my dreams far from home. Failure was not an option in my mind. I would manifest my ambitions through grit and sheer determination.

My quest to blend talent and economic freedom had officially set sail. The headwinds of adversity only made me more resolved to reach the island intact.

I was excited to be on the bustling island. The beaches were lined with white sand, the Great Salt Pond was huge, the Carnival parade was enormous, and a favorite local dish, chicken legs and johnnycakes, could be found everywhere.

When I arrived in St. Maarten, I spent my first two days just exploring the island. Coming from tiny Statia, I was completely blown away by the shops and restaurants and villagers and tourists.

I had briefly visited as a little boy, but now as a young adult, I was able to truly experience the island for the first time. I thought, *This is the place I want to be!* I was ready to embrace everything St. Maarten had to offer. The possibilities seemed endless.

All the people I admired seeing on TV, performing at the Carnival, and hearing on the radio were there—Dr. Claude Wathey, Vance James Jr., Lady Grace, Master D, Singing Olivia, and King Beau Beau. They all lived there. My brain was shouting, *HELLO, ST. MAARTEN!*

I went out and sold my seashell and bead art for about a week, but the tourists there seemed more interested in high-end costume jewelry, silver, and gold, among other things. I did not make enough to cover the cost of the trip and my daily expenses. Feeling overwhelmed and a bit discouraged, I changed course and looked for different options, *pursuing the business of life.*

I ended up remaining in St. Maarten for almost two years before returning to Statia to visit family and Uncle Bill. St. Maarten had become my new home. Uncle Bill and I lost touch. When I went back to Statia nearly two years later, we had a lot of catching up to do.

I decided to surprise him and Aunty Margie by showing up at their house unannounced. The front door was open, but no one was around. I knocked on the door and jokingly called out, "Jehovah's Witness, good afternoon! Is anybody home?"

Uncle Bill came out and exclaimed, "I know you, young man! Hey Margie, come quick, look who's here!"

It was a heartwarming welcome with lots of happy smiles and joyful faces. I also got to meet one of Uncle Bill's granddaughters, Jenny, who was 17 and visiting from New York for the first time.

Inspired by my previous crafts business, Uncle Bill had opened a little arts and crafts shop named "Hole in the Wall." He and Aunty Margie made necklaces, earrings, bracelets, and more by hand from beads, seashells, and recycled broken glass bottles. They sold these items in their store to tourists.

I told him about my life and girlfriend in St. Maarten and that I was planning to get married soon. We compared my original five-year plan to how things had actually played out over the past two years. He congratulated me on meeting some of my goals and said I should include any unfinished objectives in my next five-year plan.

I thanked Uncle Bill for his time and mentorship over the years. He replied, "The only thanks I need is your solemn promise to pay it forward. Knowledge must be passed down from generation to generation. The key to building generational wealth is ensuring that each generation does better than the one before it. You have the tools to exceed your past generation. With that comes the responsibility to push the next generation even further."

Aunty Margie was overjoyed to see me and whipped up a fresh batch of brown sugar lemonade. She insisted I stay for dinner. She was making her amazing famous garlic chicken breast with grated carrots in mashed potatoes and green beans. Just like in the Bible, it was a celebration and feast for the prodigal son who had returned home.

I spent a total of 13 years living in St. Maarten except for one year during my military service. It was a formative time in which I gained invaluable life experiences.

I lived on both the Dutch and French sides of the island, working a variety of jobs during my first five years in St. Maarten. I started in construction as a carpenter and then moved into the hospitality industry as a busboy, waiter, barboy, and bartender at various restaurants and casinos.

Though Uncle Bill had hoped I'd return to finish high school, the wisdom he imparted fueled my entrepreneurial flame. Armed with his teachings and driven by formative experiences, I set my sights on paving my own path. Rather than pursuing academics, I embraced Uncle Bill's fifth recommended option for success: learn diverse skills in the real world, then create a business matching my passion and talent. This route felt right for me.

* * *

By age 23, I was moving full steam ahead as an entrepreneur. After quitting my casino job in St. Maarten, I boldly ventured out on my own, never looking back.

Over the years, I launched businesses that allowed me to pursue my interests and live a success-filled life. These included a video rental store for movie lovers, a concert promotion company stemming from my musical passions, a cellular phone venture when that technology was still new, an investment firm focused on strategic growth, and a lively nightclub with my best friend that enlivened the island's social scene.

Though my path was unorthodox, the lessons and principles from Uncle Bill guided me each step of the way. I embraced the freedom and fulfillment of charting my own course as a young entrepreneur. Each new endeavor brought fresh opportunities to apply the business acumen nurtured in me from an early age.

During these years, I experienced so much. I had girlfriends and went through heartbreaks. I got married and divorced, becoming a stepdad along the way. I mentored teenagers, forged lifelong friendships, became a godfather, bought my first car, and built a home. The highlight was meeting my current beautiful wife of 22 years. Together, we have an amazing daughter.

As a small-town kid from Statia, working with my radio idols was a dream come true. I became pals with the legendary King Beau Beau and made radio ads alongside

Master D and Lady Grace. Through all the ups and downs, this period shaped me into who I am today.

At 30, having spent my entire adult life so far in St. Maarten, I felt ready for a new chapter. I decided to move on from the island where I had grown from a teenager into a man.

I'll always cherish the crazy days and nights that shaped me in St. Maarten. But a man shouldn't live his whole life in one place. This traveling man had lots of living left to do. So I waved goodbye, turned the page, and headed to the USA to start my next phase, *living the business of life*.

Here are some questions:

1. Did you ever make a major life transition such as moving abroad or to a new city on your own as a young adult? What was that experience like?

2. Have you ever returned to your childhood hometown after years away? What memories and feelings resurfaced?

3. What mentors from your youth had the biggest impact on shaping your path and outlook? Why were they so influential?

4. How did the wisdom and life lessons you gained in your younger years guide your decision-making as an adult?

5. If you could go back in time and advise your teenage self, what are one or two key pieces of guidance you would offer?

Pursuing the Business of Life

Transition to Adulthood

I hope that sharing the twists and turns of my early journey has sparked your entrepreneurial spirit and equipped you with valuable insights to apply to your own path ahead. By embracing uncertainty, taking smart risks, learning from failures, and persevering with passion, you can achieve your boldest dreams.

Believe in your vision. Start small and grow. Work hard and work smart. With persistence and purpose, the only real limits are those you impose on yourself.

This island boy has ventured far from home, yet the sea ever beckons beyond the horizon. But before this traveler embarks on the next leg of life's journey, I pause to share parting thoughts should my stories resonate.

* * *

To those who stand where I once stood gazing out at dreams just over the waves, take that first stroke outward with purpose. Life's currents will propel you to unexpected places, but an inner compass anchored in values will steer your course true.

For those later in the voyage seeking renewed purpose, reflect often on formative shores now distant. Let remembrances of awakening passion and grit that fueled your launch spark the flames again.

To my fellow parents and mentors, guide the next generation, but give them room to chart their course beyond the familiar harbors. Nurture their talents, then set them free to live boldly.

For anyone who found threads of wisdom in my fabric, pay it forward. Share life's lessons so those threads can be woven into tapestries more vibrant than anyone could create alone.

Keep exploring uncharted bays, venturing inward as much as outward. Live fully, love unconditionally, and laugh daily. Be present, but peer beyond the horizon. There are always new seas to sail, new lands within and without to discover, and new chapters to write in the enduring voyage called life.

In my next book, *Pursuing the Business of Life,* you'll learn about my ups and downs and my journey from ages 17 to 30, living and working on St. Maarten and grasping the 80/20 rule.

Contrary to popular belief, you can't have it all in business or life. No one gets 100% of what they want.

The 80/20 rule, though not formalized, is real. In most small businesses, 20% of customers generate 80% of revenue. In life, most people get 80% of what they desire, but by chasing the other 20%, they risk losing the 80% they already have—and most do.

This principle becomes crucial when pursuing dreams and setting priorities. If you chase every minor desire, you dilute the effort and risk losing major components of happiness. The 20% of passions and people producing 80% of joy must take priority.

Like a successful business, a fruitful life requires strategic resource allocation. Define the 20% of your goals that are delivering 80% of the value in your life and strive to achieve those first. Pursue the rest later as time and resources allow. But stay grounded in priorities to avoid ending life with more regret from dreams left unfulfilled than satisfaction from a life lived well.

Browne's Wisdom

- ❖ The horizon always beckons beyond what we can see today.
- ❖ Launch your journey with passion to propel you through life's currents.
- ❖ Nurture the seeds of greatness in your youth and watch them blossom.
- ❖ The longest journey begins with a single step... then another.
- ❖ We share one voyage called life—chart your course with purpose.
- ❖ Persevere because dreams await those bold enough to live them.
- ❖ Where we start need not define where we end up.
- ❖ Calm seas never made an expert sailor. Embrace the storms.
- ❖ The heart's truest compass points to those who shaped our journey.
- ❖ Don't allow the opinion of others about you to supersede your opinion of yourself.
- ❖ Never feel ashamed or afraid to seek help when needed.
- ❖ Parents, view your children as your legacy—they are extensions of you, not just the future.
- ❖ A perceived wrong turn may simply redirect your course toward a better destination that is meant to be.
- ❖ Let go of grudges and grievances that poison the mind and spirit.

- The deepest scars often stem from wounds inflicted in our youth.
- Though the ingredients differ, we all stir together in the melting pot called life.
- Judgment Day comes for us all, but compassion saves those willing to repent.
- Having patience while focused on long-term goals helps you avoid detours down shortcuts.
- Infuse knowledge in the young so they may be wiser than your generation.
- When all seems darkest, have faith that the stars will soon reappear.

Reflective Insights

Looking back, Uncle Bill's wisdom and guidance proved more valuable than any formal education. His role modeling mattered more than any textbook lessons.

With decades behind me now, I'm thankful that Uncle Bill saw my untapped potential and invested his time in me. Few actions are more impactful than empowering youth.

While I didn't always heed Uncle Bill's advice at the time, his words have guided me through life's twists and turns. I hear his voice in my mind reminding me to reflect wisely.

Though I was bold in my youth, with maturity I've learned that even bolder dreams can be achieved through thoughtful planning and small steps.

My island upbringing instilled in me the resilience, adaptability, and grit to weather life's literal and figurative storms. This inner strength through adversity has served me well.

While business success was my priority back then, today I find more fulfillment in sharing knowledge and mentoring youth to unlock their potential.

Looking back, I realize that Uncle Bill taught me that you must fill your own cup first before pouring knowledge into others. I now strive to walk the talk.

In my youth, I saw the world in black and white. With age comes nuance. I've learned to appreciate life's gray areas.

Now a parent myself, I better appreciate the sacrifices my mother and stepfather made to provide stability in my childhood. Their discipline molded me into the man I am.

In my youth, I took some of my parents' presence for granted. Looking back, I'm amazed by my mom's resilience as an immigrant starting over and creating a better life for her kids.

My stepdad taught me skills with his hands—how to build, repair, and create. His quiet wisdom was imparted not through words but through the satisfaction of projects completed together.

When I became a parent, I understood my mother's fears and realized how hard it must have been each time I ventured from the nest toward independence.

As a boy, I saw the world as mine to conquer without limitations. Through my parents' eyes, I now know the world can be equally wondrous and perilous.

My stepdad modeled resilience, commitment, and humility. My mom embodied strength, faith, and determination. Together, their best attributes live on through me.

Rising strong after stumbling built tenacity to propel my entrepreneurial pursuits. Turning obstacles into opportunity is the alchemy that forged my path.

Young people seek adventure while their parents protect them from its dangers. I've lived on both sides now and strive to find balance in my own parenting journey.

Thank You Notes

I once asked Uncle Bill if he would ever write a book. His answer was, "I never felt the need to write a book to pass on my knowledge because true learning comes from experiences and some good old blood, sweat, and tears."

Thank you to all of the people who have always asked me, "When will you write a book?" Well, here it is.

Thank you to those who have given feedback on stories I've shared since I started this journey. Your input has been invaluable to me.

Thank you to the people in my resource circle who have pointed me in the right direction. I appreciate your guidance.

Thank you to my wife for creating the cover of this book and building my website, and to my daughter for putting up with me during this process. Your support means the world.

Thank you in advance to my book purchasers and readers for your interest, time, purchase, and support!"

*The bonus stories in **Pursuing the Business of Life** cover the time after I first left St. Eustatius for St. Maarten and returned to visit St. Eustatius for the first time in almost two years.*

The Carpenter

Most island kids want to leave their parent's home, and island parents want their kids out of the house as well. After two weeks in St Maarten, the decision was upon me. It was time for me to head back to Statia, but I did not want to leave.

Uncle Bill had connected me with a member of the Baha'i faith team on the island. The late Miss Amanda Wrighton was a grandmother who lived in a home in the hills in South Reward. It was a two-story home, and she had an apartment on the lower level that she rented, while she lived on the top level.

Miss Amanda was just a beautiful person. She was kind and content, having worked all her life and raised her kids. She was happy living out the rest of her life doing what she loved, whether it was spending time with her grandkids or sitting on the porch looking over the valley.

She also housed kids from the islands of Saba and St Eustatius who came to St Maarten for secondary and high school. The government of the island would pay her for the room and board for housing their student.

The student got a fully furnished bedroom and two meals a day. Some kids just blended in like one of her grandkids. It was a fair way for some retirees to supplement their income and for some, it was a business housing the students anywhere from 4-5 years.

I did not get a bedroom in her house, there was a room across the walkway at the back of her property. It was a simple 22 by 13-foot space split into two rooms. One room had a bed and a small dresser, and in the other room, there were two single-seat couches and a center table.

The shower and toilet were further down at the back of the property. Three plywood boards made the shower walls and a piece of tarp as a shower curtain. The shower water was filling your bucket of water and taking it in the shower. The toilet was an outhouse (if you know what I mean). No running water or flushing toilet. I remember a time of my life growing up when that was the norm, so I was in familiar territory.

Miss Amanda was doing Uncle Bill a favor by allowing me an opportunity to explore my options in St Maarten. My two-week stay was free, and she even did a large load of laundry for me and gave me some of her hot home cooking.

Two days before my two weeks ended, I dreaded going back to Statia. So, I had a chat with Miss Amanda. I gave her 100 dollars as a token of my appreciation and her kindness. Then the next day I had a business proposal for Miss Amanda.

Being the handyman for some of my senior clients on Statia taught me that elderly people love helping the next generation. When they see that you have taken the first step, they will point you in the right direction or even walk you there themselves.

I told Miss Amanda that things did not work out as well as I had hoped selling my seashell products, but I wanted to stay in St Maarten and explore other options. I asked if she would let me stay a little longer and if I could pay her for her room.

Miss Amanda said, "Sure you can stay another two weeks for free and after that, you can pay me $80 a month by the fifth of each month." I was excited! We shook hands, and it was a deal.

Next was to find a job in St Maarten that could pay my way and save money so I could advance myself. So, I went out on the road and checked local businesses looking for a job, I tried supermarkets, restaurants, car rentals, gas stations, and construction sites. I needed a job.

After three days, I had not found work. I had to walk about a half mile up and down every day, sometimes twice a day. I remember Uncle Bill telling me, "If you don't have a job, then you have plenty of time to look for a job. Make it your job to find a job. Dress for the job you are seeking and be ready to start right away."

At the time, St Maarten was in a construction boom, and at a construction site in the Pelican area, the foreman told me I had to come early in the morning if I wanted to find work. All the men would come here in the morning, and the contractors or their foremen would announce what they were looking for.

So the next day, I woke up early and took the bus heading in that direction. I saw 40 to 50 men looking for work. There were painters, electricians, plumbers, carpenters, masons—men of all skills.

Suddenly a man came out and said, "I need three carpenters for one week," and five or six men said "Hey, me." They all had their tools and were ready to work. I was not prepared; I was there with two empty hands. Then another man shouted, "I needed 6 laborers for 3 days" and about 10 men raised their hands.

It took about 30 minutes for all the jobs to go that day. I needed a plan, so I took a deep breath and thought about what my skills were, what job would be easiest to get, and what tools I would need to buy. As I walked around the area, I saw the big need seemed to be laborers, carpenters, and masons.

I went into town to a hardware store and bought a measuring tape, a handsaw, a square, and a hammer. When I got home Miss Amanda said, "Looks like you got a job, son? When do you start?" I said, "Not yet, Miss Amanda, but I will find one tomorrow."

Uncle Bill always said, "Chance favors the prepared," so I prepared today to increase my chances tomorrow. She said

"If you are looking for construction work, you should go to Pelican Key. I heard there is lots of work there."

The next morning, I got up at 5:30 a.m., got ready, and walked down the hill, tools in hand. I took the bus and got to the staging area by 6:40 a.m.. There were about 7-10 men there waiting already. I was in the front of the line that day, and, as the saying goes, "The early bird gets the worm." I thought to myself, 'With my tools in a carry bag, as of today, I'm now a carpenter.'

A man came out and spoke in a funny accent: "I need a carpenter to work with me full time." I, along with two others, put up our hands. He looked over, and I said, "I got all my tools right here." He said, "Ok, let's go."

He said, "My name is Arnold." I said, "I'm Gramey." I asked, "Where are you from? I can't place your accent." He said, "I'm from South Africa. I sailed halfway across the world on my boat with my wife and we live on our boat in the lagoon."

As we walked up, I told him a little bit about Statia and my change of plans after my seashell products did not sell in St Maarten. I wanted to stay so I decided to get a job and pay my way.

"How much do you pay per day and when do you pay?" *The norm at the time for construction workers was to get paid a daily rate and get paid every fortnight (every other week).* Arnold said, "We will work from 7 a.m. to 3 p.m., including

30 minutes for lunch, Saturdays from 8 a.m. to 12 noon, and I'll pay $400 per week every Saturday."

That was a pretty good deal for me. I was a 17-year-old kid straight out of Statia making $400 a week in 1986. Wow!

Arnold was a subcontractor for the bigger contractors who built condos, timeshares, and large homes. The front or rear patio work was subcontracted to him. Arnold and I worked together as a team.

After a few weeks of working, some of the other workers in the area asked me, "Why do you work for that man?" I said he gave me a job. They replied, "He is a racist South African." I had never had any issues with Arnold since I worked for him. We worked and talked, had drinks after work sometimes, and he paid me every Friday.

In 1986, "apartheid" (segregation) was still the law in South Africa and Nelson Mandela was in prison. Caribbean island nations began calling for the abolishment of apartheid, including boycotting South African goods and the West Indies cricket team refusing to play matches in South Africa.

At 17, I did not have strong political opinions, and in Statia South Africa was not a regular topic of discussion. Arnold had issues keeping workers because most of the tradesmen on the island at the time were from other West Indies Islands that were championing the boycott of South Africa.

Nevertheless, I continued to work with Arnold, and about three months into our work together, he kept getting more work but was hesitant to hire more workers. So he proposed a different working relationship. He said we would work from 7 a.m. to 5 p.m. every day including Saturdays. This way we would finish jobs faster. We would get bonuses and he would give me part of the bonuses too.

"A job ain't nothing but work. If you don't want to work, don't get a job." This saying was something I learned from the first contractor I worked for as a young boy. I had nothing better to do, so I was all in. I earned $600 per week, and I got anywhere from $500 to $800 bonuses for every patio deck completed, depending on the size. The small patio decks took us a week, and the larger ones about two weeks.

Building patio decks was a very simple job if that's all you do, and that's all we did. We lay out the square or rectangle for the size. Then we dig the holes to plant the footings. We drill two holes in the footing and pass two pieces of steel rebar, putting it in the hole we dug. Then we mix concrete by hand and fill the holes. Then we went back the next day and started installing the floor, then the sides, then done.

Arnold and I worked together for about eight months until all his contracts were filled. Later, while still living in St Maarten, we would cross paths at the supermarket or events. We would have a beer and talk about our time working together. He was my first employer in St Maarten.

I saved most of my money back then, rent was cheap, and I spent all my time working. The first two weeks I started with Arnold, I created a "cost of living budget," as Uncle Bill had taught me to manage and track my money, as well as opened a bank account at the Bank of Nova Scotia. After working with Arnold for nine months, I had saved $12,400.

My first real-world budget

```
                        1986
    Income  Description  Expence  Description
    $400    work pay     $80      Rent
    $400    work pay     $20      Light
    $400    work pay     $90      Groceries
    $400    work pay     $80      Lunches
                         $80      movies
                         $15      Deodorant
                         $40      hair cuts
                         $80      Cloths
                         $40      Laundry
                         $40      buses

    $1600    —           $565
            $1035
          Save $800
       Pocket Change $235
```

Moving on

I took a little over a month off after working with Arnold. I got to know my neighbors and went to the beaches. I started making friends in St Maarten, some of whom I still communicate with today, even though we have all left the island. I played basketball in the street at the bottom of the hill with fellas from the neighborhood. I had come out of my shell and lowered my guard. I was in love with St Maarten, it was my new home.

When it was time to get back to work, I did not want to do any more back-breaking construction jobs. One of the guys I played basketball with worked for a beverage wholesaler, Vance James and Sons, and they needed some extra hands. I went down to their office the next day and interviewed for the job.

The manager, Vance James Jr., was one of the people I admired as a boy living in Statia. He was also the leader of the opposition political party in St. Maarten at the time. I got the job on the spot.

It was about 8 a.m. and the trucks had not hit the road yet. So I was assigned to my friend's truck, and we were loaded up and ready to hit the road by 10 a.m. I worked there for about three months. It was a fun job being out on the road and getting to know the island from different areas and perspectives.

One of my coworkers worked in a casino bar and they needed a barboy. He asked me if I was interested in an evening job. He worked two jobs and said I could do the same. The barboy job would be from 9 p.m. to 4 a.m.—no way would I do both jobs.

I told him I would leave the distributor's job if the barboy job paid better. Even though I liked this job, I was used to earning $400 a week and this job paid $170 a week, plus it was manual labor. He said I would make about $260 a week but get paid every other week. With my personality, I could get lots of tips to add to it. I was ready to move on.

I started the casino job that Friday and resigned from Vance James and Sons that Monday. I loved the casino ambiance—the women, the glitter, the money, and—did I already say the women? Up to that point, I had never worked in a bar or a casino. The only drinks I knew how to mix were rum and coke, gin and tonic, and vodka with orange juice.

I got a 90-day contract with an option for renewal. Three bartenders worked there full-time. I was the extra help for the peak of the season.

My job was to set up and stock every evening and fill the soda station for the waitresses on the floor. But I was the new kid. They left me alone in the bar and hung out back relaxing, as they worked two jobs and needed the extra rest. That allowed me to learn to mix more drinks, which I did. With my personality, I made lots of tips. I was able to add to my savings and still enjoy life.

In the three months I spent there, I left as a rookie bartender. I even created a drink—I called it the "G-Tail": Hennessy with Ponche Kuba shaken with ice, poured into a glass, and topped off with a splash of amaretto. Years later, I worked as a bartender at a local hot spot called Cats Nightclub.

My next job took me back to carpentry work, not in construction, but rather in a woodworking shop. That experience brought me back to my days learning cabinetry at GVP. The guys I worked with now were at a much higher level. I was not skilled enough to take on projects. I did more sanding and basic work. I stayed for about three or four months, then moved on.

Heartbreak Hill

I'm sure you have read or heard the story of Humpty Dumpty falling off the wall and couldn't be put back together again. When I got my heart broken on this hill, I felt like I was Humpty Dumpty. I thought this was where I started my new life in St. Maarten…this cannot be where it all ends. But let's not get too far ahead of ourselves.

After that, I got a job at the St. Maarten Beach Club Hotel and Casino on Front Street in the capital, Philipsburg. I worked as a busboy during lunch and evening dinner shifts, and I loved it. I had a job interacting with tourists, and I was back working in a uniform.

I was about three months into my busboy job when I met the girl who would break my heart into more than 100 pieces.

Jen was the older sister of a student from Saba who lived at Miss Amanda's house. She had been there about a week or so when we first said "Hi and Hello."

Jen had completed high school in St. Croix and since I had spent time in St. Croix too, we had things and places in common to talk about right from the start.

Jen had rented a room from Miss Amanda, just like her brother was doing... Even though there were three doors and a walkway between us, Jen was the girl next door. Jen was looking for work but had not found anything yet when we started talking. I promised to help her ask around.

Within days we were spending nights together and waking up at 5 a.m. to sneak her back into Miss Amanda's house before anyone noticed. We were like two dogs in heat, and I couldn't wait to get off work each day and see her. I was in love.

At work, the daughter, of the property owner, told me she liked my personality and thought I would be good at working at the front desk. She asked if I was interested in that position. I told her my girlfriend was looking for work too, and I would prefer if she got the front desk job and I could wait for a bartender or waiter position to become available

My boss said, "Great, Gramey, have your girlfriend come in tomorrow at 3:30 p.m. Tell her to bring all her papers. I will interview her myself."

I got off work and it felt like I floated up the half-mile hill home. When Jen came over and I gave her the good news, I told her to arrive 20 minutes early. My boss was impressed with her grades and personality and hired Jen on the spot. As she walked by, my boss said, "You have a nice girlfriend, Gramey, and she is smart too. How long have you guys been together?" I said, "Three weeks."

My boss replied, "Gramey, three weeks and you gave up a promotion for her? Wow, I hope she knows how lucky she is to have you supporting her. By the way, Gramey, she will be starting tomorrow."

I was grinning from ear to ear. I could have been more excited for Jen than she was for herself. I went home after work that evening and we were both so excited. She was happy to get a job and I was happy to have gotten it for her. It was like we were on our honeymoon.

Jen had her first day, then the next, and she was able to work at the front desk all by herself after her first week. Every time our eyes locked, we would smile like 12-year-olds having their first crush.

Then the next week our shifts got in the way. Jen was coming to work when I was leaving. By her third week, the chatter around the hotel was about the new girl—my girl.

Then one day as I was rushing home after work to get to see her before she left, I hurried up the hill. To my shocking surprise, there was the waiter holding hands with Jen, just starting their walk down the hill. They just casually walked past me as if I wasn't even there. For some reason, all I did was watch them walk by, as if part of it was not real.

It felt like I was dreaming. Why didn't words come out of my mouth? The man was my supervisor, and he knew that was my girlfriend. Why would they be holding hands? I went to my room, took a shower, and tried to process it. I considered all possible scenarios I could imagine.

I cried myself to sleep that afternoon. I then got up and went to work the next day. I saw Jen coming in while I was leaving, and she did not look my way.

I did not know what the right thing was to do. I knew her shift started at 3 p.m. and would end at 11 p.m. I decided I would wait for her on the steps when she came home so she would have to talk to me. But she did not come home that night before I went to sleep after 1 a.m.

I felt the same kind of pain I'd felt when I was locked up in jail. Why would Jen do this to me? I saw her the next morning and greeted her, but she just ignored me. At work, I heard the whispers that my waiter had taken my girl from me. My smile was wiped from my face, and I was not performing my job as I used to. By now the waiter was getting aggravated with me as well.

A couple of days after my boss called me into her office. She seemed excited as she said, "Gramey, I have another promotion for you." But as she looked into my eyes, she could see that something was wrong. "Hey, what's wrong Gramey? You don't look like your normal self. Normally I can see your smile from across the room."

She got up and closed her office door. "Have a seat and talk to me, Gramey. Tell me what's going on."

I sat down and started crying, then gathered myself together and told my boss the full story of what happened with Jen and the waiter.

My boss said, "Do you want me to fire her? I will. She is still on probation and only got the job because of you." I said no, that it was okay. We lived in the same place so I would be seeing her every day anyway.

"So, what are you going to do?" my boss asked. I said I would have to find a new place to live so I didn't have to see them together.

"But you will still work with both of them," she remarked. I said I would have to find a new job too.

"No, you don't have to do that. I can fire her," my boss insisted.

She then suggested I take the rest of the day off and come back tomorrow when we could talk some more about it.

The next few days I stayed in the house until I ran out of food. This was the first heartbreak I had ever experienced. I felt like my heart was shattered into pieces, and Jen had taken some of those pieces with her. They were gone forever. How would I ever put my heart back together without them? Now I can sympathize with Humpty Dumpty. If he was here, I'd tell him I know exactly how he feels.

I remembered my conversation with Uncle Bill who told me "The world is not fair, and experience will come at the cost of innocence." This is what he meant. The pain superseded any anger, and the love in my heart tamed any fury I might have felt.

I never went back to my job, not even to say goodbye or collect my last paycheck. I think my boss probably knew by then that I was gone for good. I was not coming back.

I decided to start looking for a new place to stay. I would need to buy a bed, a refrigerator, pots and pans—all the starter necessities when getting a new apartment. Uncle Bill was right: "Reality truly changes things." Sometimes all we can do is accept it, adapt, and move on. "It's okay, I can do this," I told myself.

I took a shower, got dressed, walked down the hill, took a bus, and went into town. The idea was to find an apartment close to town. In time, I would also need to find a new job, but securing an apartment was the priority.

I soon realized just how expensive apartments were that day in Philipsburg. As I was leaving a building, I thought might have vacancies, I saw a man approaching. I asked him if he knew if there were any apartments available there.

He told me he did not live there but had come by to find a former employee to work at a cocktail event the following afternoon. I mentioned that I was not currently working, so I could do it.

He introduced himself as Rene and asked, "Do you have black pants and a white shirt?"

I said yes, from my last job.

"Then be at the Portofino Restaurant at 4 PM tomorrow," he replied.

After that first event, I worked on three more events for Rene that week. Keeping busy helped distract my sad thoughts; the work was good for me.

Rene was the owner of the Portofino Restaurant on Front Street in Philipsburg. Event work paid $50 cash for 4 to 5 hours. It was easy money and a pleasant diversion.

After about six events, Rene asked if I wanted to work for him full-time in the restaurant. He needed a waiter to work lunch and dinner shifts. I happily accepted what felt like a seamless transition from my former busboy role.

I stayed at Amanda's house for about another three months before leaving. Work became like therapy for me. At the restaurant, I was out of my shell, distracted from brooding thoughts. I had my "customer service smile" switched on as I joked and talked with strangers, earning good tips.

But after work, I retreated to being this reserved Statia boy going back to his small studio on Heartbreak Hill.

I didn't cross paths with Jen or her boyfriend often. Or maybe I saw them but chose not to notice. I put my shattered heart back together as best I could with the pieces I had left. The missing pieces Jen took were slowly growing back with time.

No looking back

Then one Friday evening on crowded Front Street, it happened—a girl caught my eye. When she noticed me staring, she turned and spoke up. "Hey you, stop staring! Where are your manners? Can't you at least say hello?" I smiled back and looked her in the eyes. "Hi," I offered shyly.

"You're kinda cute, what's your name?" she asked.

"I'm Gramey," I replied.

She said, "I'm Junior."

"What kind of name is Gramey?" she scoffed.

I said, "You have a boy's name. I have a friend we call Junior."

"Now you have a boyfriend and a girlfriend with the same name," she said.

I laughed. It was the first time I'd genuinely laughed outside of work since my heartbreak.

She explained her name was spelled Junia. I thought to myself, 'Yeah, I like this Junia girl.'

Junia had migrated from the island of Dominica and was living with her older sister in an area called the Dutch Quarter. She was 21, two years older than me. She was about 5'5" and 160 pounds, 10 of which was butt. You might not notice her approaching, but you'd certainly watch her walking away.

We started hanging out every Friday afternoon on Front Street. I even took her up to my small studio on top of Heartbreak Hill. After reaching the top, she said the place was too far away. She would not be coming back there again.

I replied, "Well, help me find a new place closer to you then!"

The next Friday when we met up, she said she had found a place going for $100 a month, just a five-minute walk from her sister's home.

We took the bus there and I checked out the rental - it was one of eight studio units, each about 12x12 feet, with four shared bathrooms down the hall. Two units were still available, one in the middle and one at the very end. I put down a deposit on the end unit and told the owner I would move in by month's end.

That Saturday, I let Miss Amanda know I had found a new apartment and would be leaving her place before the month was over.

I was working a dinner shift the next week, so I spent my mornings cleaning and setting up my new place and by the end of the month, I said goodbye to Miss Amanda and Heartbreak Hill.

Living in the Dutch Quarter was cool in the late eighties, even though it had a reputation for criminal activities. Everyone knew everyone and the criminals generally left locals alone. I felt safe night and day and did not worry. But if you were looking for trouble, the Dutch Quarter had plenty.

When working dinner shifts on weekends, I would pass by Cats Nightclub on my route home. One night, the owner asked if I was a waiter or bartender. He needed a bartender on Friday and Saturday nights. I thought I could handle both and took the gig bartending alongside my full-time waiter job at Portofino restaurant.

Working in a lively nightclub brought back memories of my nights manning the bar in the casino. I loved that posh casino ambiance when I'd worked there previously. I admired the croupiers (casino dealers) and thought maybe one day I could do that job too.

One day while reading the paper, I saw an ad that croupier training classes were starting soon at a nearby casino. I jumped at the chance and signed up right away. The eight-week program consisted of hour-long lessons five days a week after work. After training, if you passed all the testing, you got a six-month croupier contract with the casino.

I spoke with my boss, Rene, about doing the training and continuing the lunch shift for the next eight weeks. He agreed to the arrangement so I could gain this opportunity while keeping my job. I had some vacation time and took a quick trip back to Statia. When I returned, I dove right into the casino school eagerly.

In the first class, the instructor provided an overview of game concepts, which I quickly grasped. With my knack for math, I loved all aspects of it.

I got a used deck of cards and bought a stack of $1 chips to practice with at home. After 3 weeks, I started getting the opportunity to apply my skills in live blackjack games after lessons. By week five, I was the first trainee hired on a contract as a croupier for Caribbean Stud Poker and Blackjack.

I worked most of my six-month contract with the Seaview Casino before leaving for a better opportunity at the Pelican Casino. I spent almost four years there and learned and acquired the skills for Roulette and Craps.

The next year, I purchased my first car and we moved to the French side of the island, to an area known as the "French Quarter and never looked back.

To be continued....